Snippet Sensations

FAST, FUSIBLE
FABRIC ART FOR
QUILTED OR FRAMED
PROJECTS

Cindy Walter

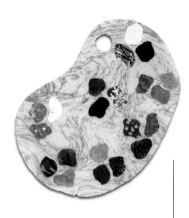

Snippet Sensations:
Fast, Fusible Fabric Art
© 1996 by Cindy Walter.

Krause Publications
700 East State St.
Iola, WI 54990-0001
715-445-2214
www.krause.com

Please call or write for our free catalog of publications. Our toll-free number to place an order or obtain a free catalog is 800-258-0929 or please use our regular business telephone 715-445-2214 for editorial comment and further information.

ISBN: 0-87341-803-4

Library of Congress Catalog Card Number: 99-61242

Acknowledgments

My life has been a whirlwind this past year. Writing this book, making Snippet Art projects, and teaching a variety of quilting classes has kept me busy! A strong support team gave me many hours of joy during the journey. Thanks and appreciation to:

≈ My Snippet Art workshop students, for having faith in my ideas and venturing into an area of textile art that was uncharted. There wasn't room in this book for every project they produced over the past few years. The editors had a hard time selecting the works to include. I am thankful for each and every one of those students.

≈ Mary Beth Mills for convincing me to take my ideas to a publisher and for the many hours we spent brainstorming new ideas and quilting patterns.

≈ The companies that had faith in my project: Fiskars Scissors supplied me with the fabulous Softouch and Micro-Softouch Scissors, and rotary equipment. Hoffman of California, Northcott/Monarch, Benartex, Shades, and Alaska Dyeworks gave me generous supplies of their beautiful fabrics that I used in many projects shown throughout this book. Warm Products gave me an endless supply of Steam-A-Seam 2. This revolutionary fusible webbing takes half the work out of fusing. Without it I would never have made my production deadlines.

≈ The local quilt shop owners who, from the very beginning, trusted my teaching ability: The Loft in Issaquah, Calico Basket in Edmonds, and In The Beginning in Seattle.

≈ And most importantly, my family and friends—they were my best critics. My family put up with my endless hours of work and understood when I said, "I can't talk right now." My friends were patient and helpful, encouraging me through each deadline. A special thanks to Lahiri, who drew several of the line drawings, and to Diana Morrison for endless hours of support.

Now back to my true passion, teaching the great art of quilting and, of course, Snippet Art!

> *I would like to dedicate this book to my late grandmothers, Lucille Draper and "Kitty" Gauger. They gave me my introduction to the world of quilting. I deeply miss both of them; their presence will remain with me always.*

On the Cover

Front Cover: *The Kiss* and *Water Lilies at Giverny* by Cindy Walter.

Back Cover: *Soaring Eagle, Mt. Rainier,* and *Wild Dolphins* by Cindy Walter.

Contents

Featured Works
(Alphabetical by Title)

Preface

When I first presented the Snippet Art™ technique to friends, several of them said, "This looks difficult to me . . . I'm not that creative or artistic." This, of course, was before they had tried the technique. Then one of them came up with a great idea. She suggested that four or five of the staff and I create a project inspired from one design image. She wanted to see how easy or difficult each person would find this technique. We searched for an image we all liked and came across a card featuring a lovely watercolor of a Christmas wreath painted by Rita Yeasting of Seattle, Washington. Everyone agreed this would be a great project to try using the Snippet technique. We were each curious about how the others would interpret and recreate the wreath in fabric.

A few weeks later the staff and I got together, each bringing her own fabric stash. Inspired by the card, we began creating our individual projects and the results astounded us. The foremost thing that became obvious to everyone, was that this technique was fun, easy, and fast. Each of our projects was at least half finished by the time we left just a few hours later. The five projects were completely different from one another. Each person's sense of color and way of manipulating the snippets produced very different results. No one duplicated the original wreath exactly, and several of the finished projects barely resembled it. This didn't matter. All our projects turned out to be unique and charming. This was the second important discovery. Regardless of how one translates or creates a design, most likely the results will be beautiful. To see for yourself how our experiment turned out, review the photographs of the original card and the five "test" wreaths on pages 75–76.

PART I

Introduction

Author's Introduction

My friends consider me a traditionalist in the quilting field. I teach many classes on the time-honored techniques of hand piecing, hand applique, and hand quilting. These friends wonder how I could have invented and refined the contemporary technique of Snippet Sensations. Even though the traditional ways passed down by our grandmothers are dear to my heart, one day I had an urge to paint on my quilt—with fabric!

The concept of painting with fabric was extraordinary to me. I had wanted to learn to oil paint for several years, but felt intimidated. Painting with a brush seemed impossible—I could never turn dabs of paint into an image. The idea of "painting" with fabric came to me as I lay in bed experiencing one of my creative spells of insomnia. Maybe I could paint with dabs (snippets) of fabric? Fabric is a medium I love and understand. *Autumn Trees,* page 42, was the result of my first experiment with the Snippet technique.

I decided to study the work of Impressionist artists and came to realize that I could create similar impressionistic pictures, not with paint—but with fabric! During one of my "addicted to reading" moods, I read Claude Monet's life story. He strove for perfection, and this fascinated me. He painted the same scenery repeatedly until he felt completely satisfied with his work. This meant capturing the image on canvas in different light exposures and during different seasons.

Monet repeatedly painted images of the gardens and water lily pond at his home in Giverny, France. He translated the same images hundreds of different ways and the results were all beautiful. Monet's style and persistence inspired me profoundly.

Giverney by Claude Monet.

Water Lilies by Claude Monet.

I reflected on my technique and went on to produce *Water Lilies at Giverny,* page 52. Not stopping with impressionism, I experimented with artistic styles from realist to abstract, and discovered that each style was easy to express in fabric. Every snippet of fabric represented a dab of paint. Using fabric and fusible web, I could cut snippets and drop them right onto a fabric foundation. Thus the Snippet Sensations concept was born!

I had never considered myself creative or artistic even though I could easily copy ideas and images. However, the more I experiment with new Snippet designs, the more I feel my creativity surface. I now believe that each of us has a creative side.

At first I felt intimidated when beginning a Snippet project. You may feel this way, too, but don't be misled! As each new project took shape, the process became easier. Snippets began to flow from my scissors. With each additional layer of snippets the project took on a life of its own. Snippet Art became an easy way for me to be successful in the world of art and contemporary quilting.

Snippet Sensations is a limitless technique. Since we are artists, nothing is "right or wrong." Start by reading through the process and completing one of the step-by-step projects. Or use the techniques in this book to create your own original masterpiece. Welcome to the world of Snippet Sensations!

The Seine by Pierre Auguste Renoir.

Wheat Field by Vincent Van Gogh.

About This Book

This book will teach you how to create your own unique Snippet Sensations projects. The three parts of this book guide you through the Snippet technique: Part I introduces you to the world of Snippet Art; Part II provides complete information about each step and the supplies needed; and Part III contains three exciting projects with step-by-step instructions.

Part I Here you will become acquainted with terms and concepts. The Glossary defines the terms used in this book. Several, including "snippets," are new to the world of fabric. The General Supply List, included in this section, tells you what supplies you need. However, because the supplies are closely tied to the technique, do not collect or buy any supplies until you completely understand the process, which is described in Part II.

Part II This section helps you select your supplies and teaches the Snippet technique. It is broken down into 14 steps that guide you through the process. If you are anything like me, you might be tempted to skim through and not completely read each step. However, there is valuable information throughout that will help ensure the success of your projects.

You will have many choices when it comes to supplies. I've provided guidelines for making these decisions, along with my preferences. There are also choices in the general technique. Reading completely through this section allows you to make the best choices for your projects.

Gallery Use the photographs in the Gallery for inspiration and direction. Look closely at the photographs and study the colors and depth in each project. I have pointed out several specific design techniques the artists used in their works; these tips will help you create similar effects in your own work. Once you are familiar with the Snippet technique, you can effortlessly duplicate these designs and create your own as well.

Part III Step-by-step instructions are included for three Snippet Sensations projects: *Festive Wreath, Soaring Eagle,* and *Italian City.* Each project features a different background style. Even though you may decide not to create any of these projects, reading through this section will increase your understanding of the general Snippet process.

Appendix At the back of this book are two valuable lists: "Supply Sources," to help you locate any hard to find supplies, and "Suggested Reading," to help you learn or brush up on skills such as quilting and embellishing.

Treat this book as a one-on-one workshop between you and me. Improvise on or personalize the designs included. Remember, when the creative juices flow from within, there is no "right or wrong"! If you should feel discouraged about the development of a design, reflect on this:

Creativity is like opening the mailbox.
Sometimes it seems empty; at other times it is full of great surprises!

> **Tip**
>
> While it's human nature to want to dive in and start right away, I strongly recommend that you read Part I and Part II before beginning.

Glossary

You may already know the meanings of the terms in this glossary, but until now they usually have not been associated with fabric or quilting. This glossary defines the terms as I use them to describe and teach Snippet Sensations.

Background Styles The background is the backdrop for the main images or design elements in a project. Snippet projects are created with one or a combination of the three background styles:

Exposed Foundation The piece of fabric used for the foundation is chosen with the idea that parts of this fabric will be left uncovered. The color and pattern of the fabric become part of the design. For an example of this style see *Festive Wreath,* page 69.

Panel Background This background style uses several larger pre-fused fabric panels to cover the foundation fabric. These panels create a background for the major design image or images. For an example of this style see *Soaring Eagle,* below and on page 78.

Snippet Background This background style uses snippets (small pieces of pre-fused fabric) to completely cover the foundation fabric. This creates a more finely shaded or textured backdrop for the major design elements. For an example of this style see *Italian City,* page 86.

Foundation fabric

Sky panel
(this is the most distant element in the depth order; it is placed first.)

Predetermined snippets
(cut in curved feather shapes)

The eagle is the closest design element in the depth order; it is created last

Hill panel
(the closest element of the panel background)

This picture shows some glossary terms at work. For more about this project, see "Project 2: *Soaring Eagle*" in Part III.

Fusible web

Random Snippets

Predetermined Snippets

Theme Snippets

Depth The imaginary distance created between the objects in the foreground of a picture and those in the background. Snippet Art projects are created in depth order: elements in the distance (background) first, and closer elements (in the foreground) last.

Fabric Palette The fabrics used to create the design images. These fabrics are pre-fused to a fusible webbing product and cut into snippets or into panels. The fabrics can come from your scrap bag or be bought specifically for each project.

Foundation The piece of fabric onto which layers of snippets and panels are adhered to create Snippet projects. This can be compared to the canvas on which an artist paints. There are three basic background styles that affect the choice of fabric used for the foundation.

Fusible Web A two-sided, fusing film used to adhere two pieces of fabric together by ironing, rather than sewing. There are many brands of fusible web. Each has different characteristics. My observations and recommendations are in Part II, page 24.

Makeshift Ironing Board A piece of cardboard, without creases, cut larger than the finished size of a project. This is used in place of a commercial ironing board. Makeshift boards protect tables and other surfaces and allow a project to remain flat and stationary. Most commercial ironing boards are too narrow to allow an entire project to lay out flat.

Panels Panels are pre-fused fabric pieces cut into larger, predetermined shapes such as hills, mountains, or fields. Fabrics with special designs, theme prints, or beautiful hand-dyes work exceptionally well for panels.

Pre-fuse To adhere fusible web to the wrong side of fabric before you cut the fabric into smaller shapes. Some brands of web use heat to pre-fuse. Others are sticky to the touch and simply adhere to the fabric with pressure.

Snippets Pre-fused fabric cut into shapes. Snippets are the "building blocks" of Snippet Art. There are three types of snippets: Random Snippets, Predetermined Snippets, and Theme Snippets.

    Random Snippets Shapes cut from the pre-fused fabric in an unplanned and arbitrary manner.

    Predetermined Snippets Pieces of pre-fused fabric cut into specifically planned shapes instead of randomly cut shapes, for example, the fence posts in *Behind the Picket Fence,* page 58. Predetermined shapes can be drawn on the webbing paper liner first or just cut with a definite shape in mind.

    Theme Snippets Theme fabrics have images or scenery printed on them. Theme snippets are pieces cut from pre-fused theme fabrics. See *The Domestic View,* page 20, for a project made almost exclusively with theme prints.

Snippet Art The term I invented for projects created with pre-fused pieces of fabrics, cut into random or predetermined shapes, and fused onto a foundation fabric.

General Supply List

Design source
(e.g., sketch)

Below is a brief list of the supplies you may need for a Snippet Sensations project. There are many choices to make when collecting the supplies. The amounts and best choices can vary according to the Snippet style. As you progress through the steps in Part II, detailed explanations are provided to help you choose the appropriate supplies to create your Snippet project.

Item	Description
Design Source (see Step 1)	An image you use as a guide and inspiration while creating your Snippet projects.
Foundation Fabric (see Step 2)	2" larger all around than the finished project size. Color is determined by background style.
Fabric Palette (see Step 3)	Fabric scraps or purchased fabrics in all the colors and shades needed to create your Snippet design.
Fusible Webbing (see Step 4)	Two-sided fusing web. Approximately ½ yard for each square foot of the project size.
Steam Iron (see Step 5)	Used to fuse snippets, and pre-fuse fabrics if traditional web is used.
Ironing Board (see Step 5)	Because of the fusing glue, an ironing board with an old cover is advisable, or use a cardboard "makeshift" ironing board.
Scissors (see Steps 9 & 10)	Must be sharp and comfortable. Use large scissors for panels and small scissors for detailed Snippets.
Embellishments (see Step 12)	Optional. Includes ribbon, charms, fabric pens, beads, and buttons.
Quilting Supplies (see Step 13)	Optional. Includes border and backing fabrics, batting, sewing machine, thread, and needles. Needed for quilted projects only.
Framing Supplies (see Step 13)	Optional. Can include mounting board, mat, and frame. Needed for framed projects only.

Note For more information about each supply item, read the corresponding step in Part II, "The Process."

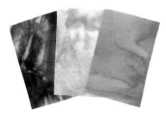

Fabric palette
(e.g., scraps)

Fusible web

Iron and
makeshift ironing board

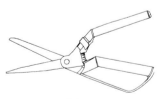

Scissors
(e.g., Fiskars Softouch)

Embellishment
(e.g., charm)

Process Preview

Snippet Art is created by following a sequence of easy steps that incorporate fusible web and assorted fabrics. Each step is discussed in detail in Part II. The supplies needed for each step are also described in Part II, along with guidelines for making your selections. For this reason, it is important to read Part II thoroughly. Here is a brief summary of the Snippet Sensations process:

1. Choose a design. Design sources and inspirations are limitless!

2. Choose a background style that suits your design. The background style determines what to use as the foundation fabric. The fabric can be partially exposed, covered with panels, or covered with snippets. Choose and prepare the foundation fabric.

3. Collect the fabrics needed to create your design (the fabric palette). Color, pattern, and texture are important considerations.

4. Choose a fusible web that suits your creative style. Each brand has different characteristics and different "how to" instructions.

5. Gather the ironing equipment you will be using. If you prefer, create a makeshift ironing board from a piece of cardboard.

6. Pre-fuse the fusible web to the wrong side of the palette fabrics.

7. Clean up the pre-fused fabrics by trimming away frayed edges, loose threads, excess glue, and fabric areas with no glue.

8. Determine the design depth and the order of the snippet layers. The design elements will be placed onto the foundation in their order of depth, starting with the farthest and ending with the nearest.

9. Create the background.

10. Cut and fuse the snippets onto the background, creating the design elements.

11. Review your progress. What else does the project need?

12. Embellish the project, if desired.

13. Finish the project by framing or quilting it.

14. Clean your equipment and store excess supplies.

Once you begin cutting and fusing the snippets, you can complete some projects in a few hours. Start your first project by reading through Part II and gathering the necessary materials and tools. You can use your own design inspiration or follow one of the step-by-step projects in Part III. I am sure the results will delight you. Once you've been through the Snippet Art process a couple times, you'll be delighted to find how fluid and versatile the technique really is.

The Secret

The secret to being successful with Snippet Sensations is to *just start and keep going.* That's right, just get started! After you've passed this hurdle, I can guarantee that you will enjoy yourself and have success with this technique. Snippet Sensations is easy and fun once you understand the process. Start with a smaller project and work your way up to a magnificent masterpiece.

PART II

The Process

1 Choose a Design

Design inspirations for Snippet Sensations can come from many sources. You may already have a design idea for the first project. (Good for you—I'm envious!) You can use a picture, draw a design, or use an image from your mind to guide you as you create Snippet Art. Start collecting pictures and making notes of the visual stimulation that surrounds you. Anything that catches your eye could eventually be a Snippet project! You can recreate almost any type of image, including scenery, portraits, still lifes, or modern art masterpieces.

Some of my favorite sources for design ideas include calendars, vacation photos, greeting cards, postcards, and postage stamps. While browsing through books at the library, I always find inspirational pictures. Books on art, animals, flowers, and nature are wonderful. Travel books often contain beautiful scenery shots.

Earth & Moon by Patti West, 19˝ x 19½˝.

Even the simplest object can inspire a beautiful Snippet design. One of my students copied the design from her favorite coffee mug. (See *Earth and Moon*, left.) A country magazine inspired another student to create *Garden Door,* page 62. For a fun, unrestrained project try an abstract, modern art piece, such as *Canyon Waterfall,* below left.

Great artists such as Renoir, Manet, Klimt, and Monet inspired several of the projects in this book. For example, see the two "Little Girls" on the opposite page. Studying and recreating works of the great masters is a fun lesson in art and history.

Design Considerations

After browsing through some books or cards, you may have so many design ideas that you cannot decide which one to use. For the first few projects select less complicated designs. A picture of a single object might be a good starting place. I find scenery an easy and "forgiving" subject to translate to fabric. Adding an extra blade of grass here and there, or altering the shape of a hill does not change the overall design effect. Still life images are also easy to translate to Snippet Art, but require a bit more accuracy with the placement of the snippets. Portraits, on the other hand, are less "forgiving." Attention to detail is important to the overall design, and snippet placement needs to be precise.

Canyon Waterfall by Emily Leong Fisher, 18˝ x 14˝.

For a first project, it is best to choose a design that has high color contrast among the different design areas. If the sky, trees, and water are all shades of teal blue, it will be difficult to distinguish among the design elements in the final Snippet picture. To keep each element distinct, try a scene that uses light blues for the sky, forest greens for the trees, and deep teal blues for the water.

You will have the best results if you are enthusiastic about your subject. Regardless of how easy or difficult the image, you will be successful if you have a strong feeling for the design. Two of my students traveled 300 miles to be in my class. I was nervous when I saw that they both picked extremely difficult pictures to create. Each was a portrait of someone they deeply loved. To my amazement they both succeeded in creating wonderful projects. Obviously, both of these women were talented, but I also attribute their success to the amount of passion they had for their projects. See for yourself: *Gone But Not Forgotten* on page 59, and *Ashley's Ecstasy* on page 67.

Recap

Almost any image can translate into a Snippet project. Start with an easier design such as a single image or scenery. Images that require precise placement, such as portraits, are difficult but not impossible. Look through books, photos, and cards for design ideas. Eventually, you will see Snippet "possibilities" everywhere you turn. Then the difficulty will be selecting *which one* to do next.

Little Girl in a Blue Armchair (painting) by Mary Cassatt.

Little Girl Lounging by Renée Arns, 20 " x 22 ".

Renoir's Little Girl in the Garden by Judy Shaffer.

Girl with Parasol (painting) by Pierre Auguste Renoir.

Alert

Unfortunately, Judy's *Little Girl in the Garden* was stolen. If you should see this piece, please notify Krause Publications.

STEP 2 *Select a Background Style*

The background and design elements are built on a foundation fabric. Another way to think of the foundation is as an artist's canvas. The background, if any, is fused on top of the foundation. All the snippets that create the design are then fused to the background.

There are three general background styles: Exposed Foundation, Panel Background, and Snippet Background. The background style you choose will determine the type of fabric you need for the foundation. The task, then, is to select a background style and pick out a foundation fabric that best suits your project. Study your design and think about the different background style possibilities. Here are some factors to consider.

Owl I by Cindy Walter (Exposed Foundation).

Owl II by Cindy Walter (Panel Background).

Background Styles

Exposed Foundation

A project with an exposed foundation is fast and easy. For this background style, areas of the foundation are left uncovered and become part of the design. Therefore, the fabric color and print are extremely important. The foundation fabric needs to be considered as one of the main background elements. In Part III, the first project, *Festive Wreath*, is done with an exposed foundation. The foundation fabric is left uncovered except where it is covered by the wreath snippets.

Other examples of this style are *Cottonwoods*, page 60; *Lilacs*, page 64; and *The Mission*, page 66.

Panel Background

This style uses large pieces, or panels, of fabric to cover the foundation. The panels create the background for the design elements and completely cover the foundation fabric. This is a perfect way to produce a sense of depth or movement in the background of your picture. Panels are easy and fast to create and fuse onto the foundation. The second design in Part III, *Soaring Eagle*, is done with a panel background. The background is made with several large pieces of hand-dyed fabrics. The eagle is then made with snippets fused on top of the panels.

Other examples of this style are: *Autumn Trees*, page 42; *The Three Goddesses*, page 56; and *Wheat Country*, page 60.

Snippet Background

This style uses small snippets of fabric to completely cover the foundation, creating the background and giving a wonderful impressionistic look. Covering the entire foundation with snippets uses more fabric, but smaller pieces or scraps can be used. Except for the foundation, no large pieces of fabric are necessary. The third project in Part III, *Italian City*, is done with a snippet background. The snippets that create the city and trees are fused on top of the background snippets.

Other examples of this style are: *Wild Dolphins*, page 63; *San Juan Sunset*, page 65; and *Tropical Sunset*, page 65.

Owl III, by Cindy Walter (Snippet Background)

Background Style Considerations

When trying to decide which style best complements your design, ask yourself the following questions: What is the background of the design? Do I have a large enough piece of fabric to use for this background? (Exposed Foundation.) Is there a sense of movement in the background? Would several layers of different fabric work best for the background? (Panel Background.) Or, are there so many colors in the background that numerous layers of snippets would work best? (Snippet Background.)

In the three photographs that accompany the style definitions, an owl is the main design element. Each picture uses a different background style. Compare how the background style affects the overall design. A design can be done in any background style, but some designs are better suited to just one style. Which do you like best? Which would you choose? For your projects the choice is up to you. As you become more familiar with the Snippet technique, you may decide to combine two or more styles in a single project.

Choosing a Foundation Fabric

For the foundation, I find it easiest to work with 100% cotton fabric. Cotton reacts well to heat and fusible web. There is no need to pre-wash the foundation fabric. Ironing the fabric with a hot steam iron pre-shrinks fabrics enough for the Snippet technique. The background style is the main factor in deciding the color of fabric to use for the foundation.

Exposed Foundation

Since parts of the foundation are left uncovered, plan the fabric choice accordingly. Small or large areas of the foundation can be left open and bare. To produce a three-dimensional effect, the exposed foundation area should be the element that is the farthest in distance, for example the sky of a scenery design.

The fabric for an exposed foundation project can be any color from plain white to the colors of the rainbow. Hand-dyed fabrics, marbled fabrics, theme prints or other specialty fabrics make remarkable exposed foundations. A lovely hand-dyed fabric, from Shades Inc. Hand Dyed Textiles, was used as the exposed foundation for *Hibiscus*, page 58. Using a large piece of beautiful fabric for an exposed foundation can enhance the project and also save time.

Panel and Snippet Backgrounds

If you are going to cover the foundation with snippets or panels, a plain white cotton works well as the foundation fabric. For a completely covered foundation, I prefer a solid fabric, usually white or off-white muslin. Other solid colors could be used. Since snippets in shades of blue were used to cover the base of *For the Love of Monet,* page 64, a solid blue foundation was used. That way, in case a tiny area didn't get covered by the snippets, the blue would blend into the design and not show.

Foundation Size Considerations

The finished size of the project is completely up to you, although there are a few guidelines to keep in mind. Smaller projects are usually faster, use less fabric, and have fewer snippets than larger projects. An exception to this is miniature sized projects. It can take longer and be more difficult to cut and place the small snippets for a miniature than it would for a medium or large project.

Another consideration is whether you plan to finish the project as a picture or a quilt. If you plan to frame your Snippet Art, consider making the finished size fit a pre-made mat and frame. This saves you time and money in the long run. (For more about framing, see page 45.) Quilted projects can be any size you want, or made to a specific measurement for incorporation into a larger quilt.

To determine the measurements of the foundation fabric:

1. Calculate the finished project size.

2. Cut the foundation fabric 4″ wider and 4″ longer than the finished size. This gives you 2″ of excess fabric all around the design area.

The excess fabric will be used in different ways depending on how you choose to finish the project. If you choose to frame a project, the excess fabric can be used in the stretching and framing process. (Many professional framers require excess fabric.) Quilting a project is less restrictive, but having extra fabric is better than having too little. Excess foundation fabric also provides room for growth. In the process of being creative, the project often swells. The clouds need to reach farther into the sky, or one more row of flowers is needed across the bottom of a garden. Extra foundation fabric gives you "artistic space."

Recap

Select the background style that you feel best lends itself to your design. The foundation fabric can be anything from white muslin to beautiful hand-dyes. The fabric choice depends on whether the foundation shows or is covered with either snippets or panels. Remember to cut the foundation fabric at least 4″ longer and 4″ wider than the finished size. Steam iron the fabric to pre-shrink and remove wrinkles.

Tip

Check with your local framing and craft stores to see what size pre-made mats and frames they carry. Also make sure you can find mounting board, mat, and frame sizes that are compatible with each other.

STEP 3 *Collect Palette Fabrics*

You are now ready to prepare the Fabric Palette. This is the collection of fabrics in the colors that you need to create your Snippet Art design. Use fabrics of different types of fiber, weave, color value, and print. I particularly like using cotton fabrics in my projects. The heat of the iron permeates the glue evenly. Theme prints and hand-dyes add excitement to any project. Select several fabrics to represent each color in your design. Step 3 covers a variety of ideas and choices for color and fabric types.

Fabric Colors

To collect the colors needed, study your design source. Don't be surprised to discover you need a wider variety of colors than you first thought. For example, grass may appear green, but on closer examination it might also have shades of brown, gold, and blue. I noticed this while creating *Water Lilies at Giverny*, page 52. The original painting appeared mostly green and purple. Upon closer examination I discovered that it contains many different colors and shades. Everyone sees colors differently, so don't worry if your colors are not an exact match. With practice, determining the colors within a design image becomes easy and fun.

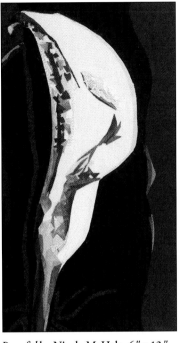

Peaceful by Nicole McHale, 6″ x 12″. Inspired by the painting *Single Lily with Red* by Georgia O'Keefe.

Solids

Solid colored fabrics produce an interesting effect. Two wonderful examples of pictures made with solids are *Garden Door*, page 62, and *Peaceful,* at right. The pictures have clear tones, as if each color of paint dried before the next color was added. For a range of shades within the same color family, I turn to hand-dyed fabrics. All the hand-dyes in *Girl Before a Mirror,* page 53, are from Alaska Dyeworks.

Monochromatic Prints

A monochromatic fabric has a pattern in shades of only one color. These prints create stunning results. *Lighthouse Rock*, at right, uses mainly monochromatic prints to create the design elements. Many of my students start with monochromatic prints and go on to experiment with multi-colored, patterned prints. Fabrics I enjoying using from Northcott/Monarch and Benartex fall into this category.

Lighthouse Rock by Jeanne Ferguson, 10½″ x 13½″.

Multi-Colored Prints

I love using fabric with loads of color and pattern. Using prints results in a textured effect that resembles brush strokes in paint. This gives another dimension to Snippet Art. As a multi-colored print is cut into snippets, the pattern becomes less pronounced. The hue (color) and value (lightness or darkness) remain, however, as the "voice" of the fabric. Many of the fabrics used in *A Mum For Mom,* at left, are multi-colored prints and enhance the overall effect.

Study your design source and make a list of all the colors. But before gathering the fabrics for your palette, there are some other choices to make. Read on.

Theme Prints and Hand-Dyed Fabrics

Theme prints and hand-dyed fabrics can be used in truly creative ways for Snippet projects. Many times you will have a very specific image you want to include in the design. Theme prints are great for this. On the other hand, hand-dyed fabrics are "fluid" and create the effect of movement.

A Mum For Mom by Marilyn Doheny-Smith, 12" x 23½".

Theme Prints

Fabrics printed with animals, objects, or scenery are called theme prints. Many times you can find a motif printed on fabric that is perfect to add to your Snippet project. This was done to create the entire scene of *The Domestic View,* at left. Many of the objects and animals were cut out of the same piece of farm fabric and fused onto the foundation. Sometimes you will look for a theme print just to add a finishing touch. In *Behind the Picket Fence,* page 58, the artist has several cats peeking out from behind the fence. She simply pre-fused a piece of cat fabric with fusible webbing, cut assorted cats out around their edges, and fused them onto the design.

Fabric with large theme prints can be treated in the same manner and used as panels. For *Wheat Country,* page 60, theme fabrics were cut into large panels and fused to the background. The mountains, the fields, and even the barn are all cut from theme prints. The fabrics were pre-fused and the desired objects were cut out and strategically placed

The Domestic View by Beverly Colson, 16" x 20".

on the background. This artist avidly collects and saves theme prints to use in the "perfect" project.

Another unique use for theme fabrics is shown in *Pink Roses,* at right. The artist pre-fused a large floral print fabric. She then cut apart the petals and fused them in layers to create a multi-dimensional look.

Fabric manufacturers release new fabrics several times a year and phase out old prints. Manufacturers don't often reprint a fabric design more than once. Since this is the case, it would be difficult, if not impossible, for you to find the exact same fabrics (particularly theme prints) used to create the projects in this book. Keep your eyes open, though. Fabric designers are always coming up with exciting, new fabrics. You are likely to find fabrics with cats or other animals, sky, water, and perhaps mountains printed on it. They will not be the same fabrics used in this book; maybe they will be better.

Pink Roses by Flo Valentine, 15″ x 12″.

Hand-Dyed and Batik Fabrics

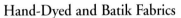

I enjoy using hand-dyed and batik fabrics in my Snippet projects. Hand-dyes, with their unique colors and variations of shading on the same piece of fabric, create an effect of light coming through, or reflection off the surface of objects. I especially like hand-dyed fabrics with a marbled effect. If you choose, hand-dye your own fabric. It's fun, but lots of work. Many fabric manufacturers are producing batiks or "hand-dye look-alikes". Several smaller companies make and sell beautiful hand-dyed fabrics. (Refer to "Supply Sources," page 93.)

Companies that produce fabrics that I like to use are Northcott/Monarch, Benartex, Hoffman of California, Skydyes, Shades Inc. Hand Dyed Textiles, and Alaska Dyeworks. *Tranquil Twilight,* on page 52, was made exclusively with Hoffman fabrics. Fabrics from Shades Inc. were used for *Hibiscus,* above right. Fabrics from Alaska Dyeworks have a more solid appearance, and their variation of color shades is unbeatable. *Girl Before a Mirror,* right, uses fabric from Alaska Dyeworks.

Hibiscus by Diana Morrison, 20″ x 18″. See also page 58.

Girl Before a Mirror (detail) by Cindy Walter. See also page 53.

Fabric Types

I like working with cotton fabrics. Since I am a long-time quilter, I have plenty of cotton fabric as well as cotton scraps. The heat of the iron evenly penetrates through cotton to the web glue. Yet, don't rule out using other fabrics in Snippet projects. Brown corduroy can create a wonderful bear in the woods; or satin would make shiny flower petals. In *Lesson in Pink,* at left, several different types of fabric were used, from linen to silk.

In my junior high school days, Home Economics was a required class. (How times have changed!) I am thankful for the sewing education. During those three years the hemline changed from 2″ above the knee, to the maxi, to the midi, to the mini, and then to the micro mini. (Wait, do I have that backwards?) I was sewing new dresses and re-hemming skirts about every six months. This training eventually gave me the courage to sew most of my clothes. Don't get me wrong; I was never the world's greatest seamstress. The point I'm making is that the best thing that remains from that training and my 25 years of garment sewing is all the fabric SCRAPS. I use the scraps of satin, raw silk, broadcloth, polyester (it was the '70s), and velour to add texture to my designs.

The only limitation on fabrics used for the Snippet technique is that they must be able to be ironed. Since lamé and other delicate fabrics cannot be directly exposed to heat, place an ironing sheet between the fabric and the iron to protect it from the heat. A good rule to follow is to test-iron any fabric to see how it responds to the fusible web, the ironing sheet, and the heat of the iron. (For more about test-ironing fabrics, see Step 6.) Another option is to treat these fabrics as an embellishment and use fabric glue or thread to adhere them later.

Lesson in Pink by Nicole McHale, 27 ″ x 24 ″. Inspired by the painting *Bleeding Heart* by Georgia O'Keefe.

Metallic and lamé fabrics

Collecting Fabrics

Fabric scrap bags are perfect for this technique. You might want to plan the color scheme around the fabrics you already have. If your scrap bag is full of shades of blue, for example, you probably have enough fabric to create an ocean scene. Share or trade scraps with a group of your "artsy" friends. This is a fun and easy way to fill in your collection with any missing colors.

Since your scrap bag is likely to contain colors that you favor, you might need to "stretch" by buying colors that you do not normally consider. As you collect scraps and new fabrics, think mainly about color. An unusual color might be the perfect accent that helps emphasize the focal point of your work. Orange is not my favorite color, but imagine how boring *Tropical Sunset*, page 65, would be if it were missing.

Amounts Needed

The amount of each fabric you need depends on the project size and the proportion of each color to the overall design. For example, a few snippets of red in a sunset would require only a small amount of fabric. If the project is small, 12″ x 18″, I would pre-fuse approximately a 2″ square of red. For a large project, 45″ x 60″, I would pre-fuse a ⅛ yard piece of red. If a design has a gigantic brown barn, you would need ample amounts of brown in several shades, perhaps ⅛ yard of six or more browns. My rule is to pre-fuse a little more fabric than I think is needed.

Pre-Washing Fabrics

I strongly recommend pre-washing the fabrics. Even though the fabrics remain crisp and bright when they are not pre-washed, some brands of the fusible web instruct you to pre-wash fabrics. They want any shrinkage to occur before the glue layer is adhered to the fabric. The amount of shrinkage in a snippet would be minuscule, but the shrinkage in a panel might be noticeable. Pre-washing the fabric is important when using Steam-A-Seam 2 double-stick fusible web. Washing away the fabric's sizing will allow the pressure-sensitive adhesive to adhere.

Recap

Closely examine your design source. Make a list of all the colors included in the design. Gather the fabrics for your palette and determine how much you need of each piece. To get a feel for how much fabric Snippet projects use, read through the Project Supply Lists in Part III. Almost any type of fabric works for Snippet Sensations projects. Cottons are the easiest to use, but other types of fabric can add texture and color effects that cotton cannot. Experiment with color and print choices. Remember, to select several fabrics to represent a color, for example, select several blues and several oranges–not just one of each. Once you collect the fabrics for your palette, take inventory. Do you have all the colors? Do you have several shades of each color? The amount of each fabric you need depends on the project size and the proportion of each color to the overall design.

STEP
4 *Select Fusible Web*

Warning!

Overheating can damage traditional web. If the web is heated too long, it loses the ability to bond one fabric to another.

Fusible web is a web-like material that has adhesive glue on both sides. When heat is applied to it, the web permanently adheres fabric to fabric. The web, depending on the brand, is also referred to as iron-on adhesive, paper-backed web, transfer web, applique web, and iron-on fabric fusing web. There are many brands of fusible web. Since each has specific instructions for the fusing process, it is important to closely follow the directions that come with the web. One of the major differences among brands is the length of time the hot iron is left in place so that the web bonds to the fabric. For this reason, I strongly recommend that you use only one type of web on a project. Ten seconds of heat may securely bond one brand of web, but for another brand this length of time could be disastrous.

Fusible Web Characteristics

The different fusible web brands have both similar and unique attributes. Read the directions carefully, experiment with several types, and choose the brand that best suits your working style. I have worked with many brands of web, including Aleene's Fusible Web™, Heat N Bond®, Steam-A-Seam 2®, and Wonder-Under®. All of these brands are reliable, quality products.

Until recently, most fusible web required two stages of ironing—one to pre-fuse the web to the wrong side of the fabric, and one to fuse the fabric to another fabric. I call these products "traditional" web. Aleene's, Heat N Bond, and Wonder-Under are in this category.

A fairly new type, Steam-A-Seam 2, is a revolutionary product. It is used differently than the traditional web products. Steam-A-Seam 2 is pressure sensitive and sticks to fabric with pressure. To pre-fuse fabrics, remove a paper liner, place the web on the wrong side of the fabric, and gently smooth it on with your hand. This eliminates the need to pre-fuse fabrics with an iron. Once you remove the Steam-A-Seam 2's remaining lining paper, snippets or panels will stick to the foundation fabric with a slight amount of hand pressure. The snippets can be picked up and repositioned. When all the panels and snippets are in place, ironing fuses them permanently in place. The web material can be removed from any unironed portions of fabric, and both the fabric and the web can be reused. If possible, I recommend that you try this wonderful product.

Choosing a brand may come down to the one that has the most characteristics you like. I buy fusible web by the yard off a bolt. I have had bad experiences with web from a folded package. When ironed, the glue does not transfer evenly to the fabric at the folded creases. Experiment!

The following chart shows the results of my fusible web experiments.

	Aleene's Fusible Web™	Heat N Bond®	Steam-A-Seam 2®	Wonder-Under®
Easy to see glue coating		✓	✓	
Paper pulls off easily	✓	✓	✓	
Needs heat to Pre-fuse	✓	✓		✓
Pre-fuse without heat			✓	
Longer heating time	✓		✓	✓
Shorter heating time		✓		
Easy to quilt through	✓		✓	✓
Unironed portions reusable			✓	

Amount Needed

To determine the amount of fusible web to buy, use the estimated finished size of your project. Approximately ½ yard is needed for each square foot of the finished project size. In other words, if a project's finished size is 2 feet by 3 feet (2 feet x 3 feet = 6 square feet), *approximately* 3 yards of fusing web is needed (½ yard x 6 = 3 yards).

Recap

Decide which brand of fusible web you want to use. I strongly recommend that you try Steam-A-Seam 2. Use the estimated finished project size to determine the amount of web to buy for your project. Read carefully through the directions that come with the fusible web to understand its special requirements. Remember that too much heat will destroy the integrity of traditional brands of web.

STEP

5 *Gather Ironing Equipment*

Snippet projects call for basic ironing equipment: a steam iron, ironing board, and some type of material to protect both these and the fabrics used for the project. Here are some recommendations.

Iron and Ironing Board

Occasionally, the fusing glue can accidentally be exposed to the iron or ironing board and adhere to them. Therefore, it is a good idea to use an old iron and ironing board for fusing. The steam iron must be in good working order. To protect the ironing board, cover it with a large piece of cotton fabric. The glue may stick to the fabric, but the ironing board cover is protected.

Another option is to create a "makeshift" ironing board. A large, flat piece of cardboard works well for this. To fuse or "set" the different snippet and panel layers, the project is ironed several times. Moving the foundation back and forth to an ironing board can disturb the snippets and send them flying. Moving the project as few times as possible prevents this from happening. To create a simple "makeshift" ironing board, cut a large piece of uncreased cardboard, slightly larger than the foundation size. Large packing boxes or the backs of paper flip charts make great ironing surfaces. Lay the foundation on top of the cardboard and you can iron the project without moving it.

Protecting the Project and Equipment

The paper liner, peeled from the fusible web, is an inexpensive way to protect your ironing board, iron, and project. This will guard against excess fusing glue. Non-stick ironing sheets (transparent, reusable pressing sheets) can also be used for this purpose. These sheets, though, are best used for protecting delicate fabrics, such as silk or lamé, from the heat of the iron. The one drawback of the non-stick ironing sheet is that it will change the ironing times necessary to pre-fuse or fuse the fabrics.

If your iron gets even slightly dirty, use some sort of pressing cloth to cover the fabric or project as you pre-fuse and fuse. This keeps the project from getting dirty. Clean the iron with a dry cloth while it is still hot. This should clean any web glue that may have melted onto the iron plate. If this does not remove all the dirt, use an iron cleaner such as Dritz Iron-Off® to clean the iron plate.

Recap

Gather and set up your ironing equipment—a steam iron and an old ironing board. Better yet, use a large, flat piece of cardboard for a makeshift ironing board. Try to situate the foundation in a permanent location so that the snippets don't "fly" away.

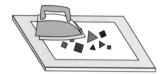

A "makeshift" ironing board allows you to iron your entire project without moving it.

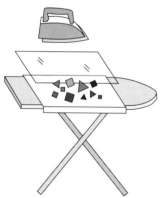

You can use the web paper liner or a non-stick ironing sheet to protect your ironing board, project, and iron.

Tip

Putting an extra layer of material, such as an ironing sheet, between the iron and the fusible web will change the ironing time required. If you decide to use an ironing sheet, experiment on a piece of "test fabric" first.

STEP 6 *Pre-Fuse Palette Fabrics*

The palette fabrics are pre-fused with fusible web before they are cut into smaller fabric pieces, or snippets, used to create a Snippet Art design. Web instructions vary for each brand so follow them closely. Check the instructions for the iron temperature setting and whether to use steam. I like to pre-fuse all of my palette fabric in one stage. This way, I do not interrupt my "creative juices" as I work on my design. If necessary, I take a break from creating to pre-fuse more fabric.

Traditional Web: Pre-fusing With Heat

One side of traditional web appears rough and shiny; the other side is covered with a layer of paper. To pre-fuse, the wrong side of the fabric is placed on the rough, shiny side of the web, then ironed. Take care not to expose the web to heat for too long. It is better to under-iron than over-iron. If you iron for a shorter time than recommended, the web can always be re-ironed. Over-ironing destroys the integrity of the glue, allowing it to melt into the fabric. If this happens, there is not enough glue to later fuse the snippets to the foundation or to other fabrics.

Steam-A-Seam 2: Pre-Fusing Without Heat

Steam-A-Seam 2 has a light coating of pressure sensitive glue on both sides of the web. This brand also has protective paper liners on both sides. To pre-fuse, simply peel off the printed liner and place the wrong side of the fabric on the web. Press firmly as you smooth the fabric over the web. The web sticks to the fabric without the heat of an iron.

Test-Ironing

To know how the different fabrics react to the web and heating length, it is a good idea to test-iron the fabrics before starting on a project. Cotton fabric usually reacts well to the web and to being heated. Other types of fabric may not react as well. Fiber content and fabric thickness may influence the ironing length and the handling of fabrics when ironed.

Heat-sensitive fabrics, such as silk or lamé, need to be protected from the surface of the iron with an ironing cloth or ironing sheet. Thick fabrics, such as corduroy, need longer ironing time to allow the heat to permeate the fabric. Fabrics such as silk need special handling. One of my students used a silk fabric that changed color and became brittle when she fused it with the iron. Test-ironing would have shown how this fabric reacted to the heat and would have alerted the student that special handling and a shorter ironing time were required.

Pre-Fusing

For traditional web products, such as Aleene's, Heat N Bond, and Wonder-Under, use the heat of an iron to pre-fuse. Read the package instructions carefully. Never over-iron traditional fusible web.

For Steam-A-Seam 2, use the pressure of your hand to pre-fuse.

To test-iron fabrics:

1. Cut a small "test swatch" (approximately 2″ x 3″) of each fabric type (cotton, silk, corduroy) you would like to test.

2. Pre-fuse the swatch, following instructions on the package of your web. If you are pre-fusing with heat, make sure to use caution and some sort of pressing cloth to protect sensitive fabrics. If you are pre-fusing with pressure (Steam-A-Seam 2), skip to instruction 4.

3. If you are pre-fusing with heat, note how the fabrics react at this pre-fusing stage. Can you peel away the paper liner? Can you see the glue? Has the fabric changed color or been damaged? Adjust your pre-fusing technique until you achieve satisfactory results, repeating instructions 1 and 2 as necessary.

4. If you have not yet done so, peel off the paper liner and cut each swatch into three strips. Label and lay out the strips on a scrap of the foundation fabric, as shown below.

5. Fuse the strips to a piece of the foundation fabric, using different ironing times for each column:

   • Fuse the fabrics in the first column a few seconds less than the recommended fusing time.

   • Fuse the fabrics in the second column as directed in the web instructions.

   • Fuse the fabrics in the third column a few seconds longer than the recommended fusing time.

6. Check each sample to see how it reacted to the pressing time. Does it stick to the foundation fabric? Did the fabric change colors? Did the fabric become brittle or change characteristics in any other way?

7. Use your findings to guide you as you pre-fuse and fuse the fabrics for your project.

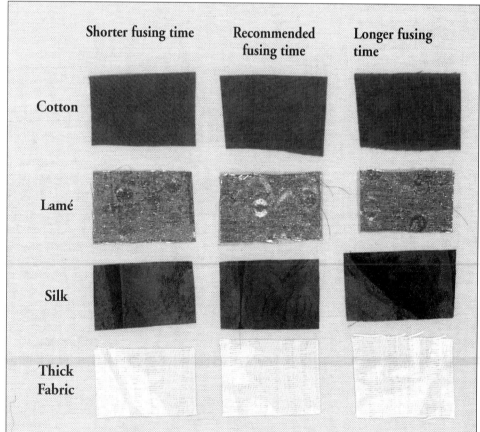

Fuse the pre-fused test swatches to a piece of the foundation fabric.

Pre-Fusing Tips

Over time, I have developed ways to make pre-fusing easier and faster.

Ironing Technique

As you move the iron from one area of fabric to the next, pick it up and set it down again. Do not slide the iron while it is on the fabric. If the iron slides across the project, it can disturb and move any unsecured fabrics.

Pre-Fusing Small Scraps

When pre-fusing small segments of fabric, several pieces can be done at the same time. Place a piece of web on the ironing board, glue side up. Next lay the small pieces of fabric next to each other on top of the web. For traditional web, iron the fabrics for just a second. This "sets" the glue to the fabric. Flip the sheet over and iron on the paper side to permanently set the glue. Iron for the recommended length of time. Setting the fabrics is an added step, but makes it easy to control all the small pieces. I use an ironing sheet (either a purchased one or a piece of the peeled off web paper liner) when I collectively pre-fuse small chunks of fabric. This keeps glue from getting on either the iron or the ironing board.

For Steam-A-Seam 2, just peel off a paper liner and smooth the wrong side of the fabric on the exposed side of the web.

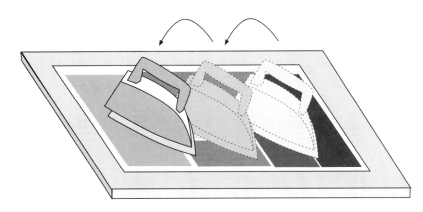

Do not slide iron on fabric. Lift up the iron to move it to a new section.

Pre-Fusing Large Fabric Pieces

For large fabric pieces, cut off the amount of web you need to pre-fuse the entire piece. For traditional web, lay the fabric, wrong side up, on the ironing board. Place the web on top, paper side up, and iron. Remember, don't over-iron. For Steam-A-Seam 2, just peel off a paper liner and smooth the wrong side of the fabric on the exposed side of the web.

Line up several small scraps and pre-fuse them all at once on one large piece of fusible web.

Web Paper

It is easy to see when traditional web has received a sufficient amount of heat to pre-fuse. The web paper turns slightly translucent. Allow the fabric and paper to cool for about ten seconds before attempting to peel off the paper liner. Use caution. It will be very hot, but cools quickly. Pull the liner off all the pre-fused pieces before use. Store the pre-fused unused pieces of fabric with the liner paper attached.

Glue Coating

With traditional web, when you peel the paper from the fabric, the glue should stick to the fabric. The glue feels like a thin coating of plastic and should evenly cover the wrong side of the fabric. If the glue sticks to the paper instead of the fabric, it did not receive enough heat. Iron again. If the glue is allowed to cool between ironing, you can continue to re-iron the web for short periods of time.

Don't Forget!

Remember to peel the web liner off the pre-fused fabrics before using. If you start cutting snippets with the liner accidentally left on, you will end up with hundreds of tiny paper-lined snippets that will not fuse to the foundation fabric. One of the few exceptions to this rule would be if you want to cut something with the fabric folded, such as a snowflake. In a case like this, leave the paper on until after you make the cuts. This prevents the glue from adhering to itself.

Save large pieces of the removed paper liner. They come in handy for several purposes. One side has a waxy coating and can safely be used as an ironing surface for the fusible web. The glue does not stick to the waxy side. Use a piece of the paper liner in place of an ironing sheet when pre-fusing fabrics. Or use the paper liner as an ironing cloth to protect an almost finished project from a dirty iron. Remember, though, iron on the paper side, not the waxy side. The wax will melt onto your iron.

Recap

Pre-fuse the palette fabrics in advance so that you can create your picture without interruption. To pre-fuse fabric with traditional fusible web, use a steam iron. Do not over-iron. Steam-A-Seam 2 adheres without heat. Follow web package directions carefully. Remember to peel the web paper liner off the fabrics before use.

STEP 7 *Trim Palette Fabrics*

This is an essential step. With scissors, trim away any frayed fabric edges, loose threads, fabric that is not coated with glue, and wisps of excess glue hanging over the fabric edges. I find it easier to do this with the web lining paper still attached. Now that we've entered the age of rotary cutters, I also use my rotary equipment (cutter and mat) to clean up the chunks of fabric.

Cleaning up the edges ensures that all the fabric has a coating of glue and will stick during the fusing stage. Trimming the frayed edges and loose threads keeps the design neat and tidy. Now the fabrics are ready for you to start creating your Snippet Sensations design.

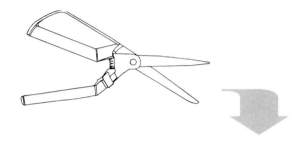

STEP 8 Determine Depth Order

Each element in a design has depth and a depth order relative to the other design elements. Depth relates to the distance between an object and the viewer—that's you. Once the depth order is established it provides the order used to create the different elements. The elements farthest away in depth are created first. The middle and closer elements are created on top of these elements.

Depth Example

Refer to the illustration below as I explore depth with you. Think about how far each element is from you. Do you see that the sky is the farthest element, the path is closer, and the flowers are the closest? The depth order of the element is the order for constructing the project. The farthest object is the first element completed and the closest object is the last. In the illustration I numbered the areas, showing the order that they would be added onto the foundation: sky (1), hill (2), path (3), grass (4), trees (5), and flowers (6). Working in depth order allows you to work with just a few colors at one time.

Study your inspiration source to determine the depth of each design element. Which component is the farthest away? Which is closest? Make a list, either a mental or a written one, to keep track of the depth order for creating the design elements and color layers. The background or object farthest away is done first. Work forward through the list and finish with the closest object.

You may find it helpful to draw the general shapes of the design elements onto the foundation before you start placing the snippets. A standard pencil is fine for this. Use the lines as a guide for the snippet placements. However, I usually do not draw placement lines, as I find this limits my freedom to create.

Recap

Study your design source to determine the depth of the design elements. The depth order determines the order to create the different areas of the design. Start with the farthest object and finish with the closest. It may be helpful to draw the general shapes of the elements.

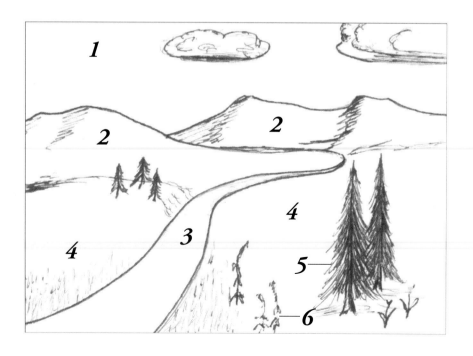

9 Create the Background

As discussed previously in the section on the background styles, page 16, no matter which style is chosen, the background is created before adding any other design elements. For *Wild Dolphins*, page 63, I first completely covered the white muslin foundation with teal and blue snippets. I then added the dolphins over this background.

Position the foundation fabric in the center of your ironing area (board or makeshift board). To keep all the snippets in place, it is helpful if the foundation is not moved until the project is completed. If the fabric piece is larger than the ironing board, I strongly suggest that you create and use a larger makeshift ironing board. Being able to view all or most of the design area at once lets you see how the sections are developing and meshing together.

Exposed Foundation

Since the foundation fabric *is* the background for this style, if the fabric is cut and pressed, you are ready to continue to Step 10, "Cut and Fuse Snippets."

Panel Background

Gather the pre-fused fabrics for the panels. Starting with the panel layer farthest away, cut each panel fabric and place it on the foundation in its depth order. When the panels are in place, set the pieces. Fuse the pieces with an iron if using traditional web. With Steam-A-Seam 2, you can either permanently fuse the panels now or leave the fusing until the snippets are fused. The panels will stay in place. The illustrations at right demonstrate placement of several background elements: a sky panel and three hill panels.

> ### "Setting" Panels
>
> **For traditional web,** use heat to permanently fuse panels to the foundation when the background is complete.
>
> **For Steam-A-Seam 2,** use light pressure from your hand to set panels in place. Iron when ready to permanently fuse them to the foundation. Fuse the project all at once when the entire design is complete.

Sky panel

First hill panel

Second hill panel

Third hill panel

Snippet Background

Gather the pre-fused fabrics for the background. Read Step 10, "Cut and Fuse Snippets," before starting a snippet background. Once you have read this section, complete the background by covering it with layers of snippets. If using traditional web, fuse the background snippets before starting the other design elements.

Recap

Position the foundation in the center of your ironing board or makeshift board. Depending on which background style you choose, either leave this base exposed, layer it with panels, or cover it with snippets. If necessary, fuse the background elements in place before starting with the foreground design elements.

In this snippet background, snippets are cut and placed for the sky, then the first hill, then the second hill, and finally the third hill.

STEP *10* *Cut and Fuse Snippets*

Snippets (small pieces of cut fabric) are the "building blocks" of Snippet Sensations. The pre-fused fabrics are cut into snippets and arranged on the foundation to create the project design. Snippets can be cut any shape or size. The snippets in *Watercolor Heart*, page 64, are small and angular. In *Wild Dolphins II* (on the following page), the snippets are larger. Both these projects use randomly shaped snippets. Snippets cut in planned shapes (predetermined snippets) are used in *Garden Door*, page 62. The leaves are cut in soft, curvy shapes. Some of the snippets on the door are cut into rectangles. These are also predetermined snippets. Theme snippets, a third type of snippet, are specific images cut from pre-fused theme fabrics. For a clearer understanding of the variety of snippet shapes, review the photos on pages 72, 83, and 90.

Scissors

Before you start cutting snippets, a few comments need to be made about scissors. A pair of sharp, quality fabric scissors make cutting the snippets rapid and effortless. Dull scissors can fray the fabric edges (as well as your nerves). If your scissors do not cut the pre-fused fabric cleanly, have them sharpened. (Or maybe it's time to buy a new pair!)

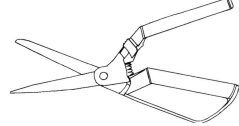

Fiskars Softouch multi-purpose scissors

Scissors are the primary tool used to create Snippet Sensations. Therefore, your scissors should be comfortable to use and not strain your hand. I prefer Fiskars® Softouch™ multi-purpose scissors. They have a spring-action handle that reduces hand fatigue. The scissors need squeezing only to cut; the spring pops the handle back open. For tiny snippets or small precision work, I use Fiskars® Softouch™ micro-tip scissors. They also have spring-action. With these scissors your hand does not tire as easily as with normal scissors. Both of these scissors can be used either right-handed or left-handed.

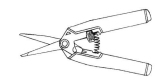

Fiskars Softouch micro-tip scissors

Snippet Shapes

Let's cover some more points about the different snippet shapes: Random Snippets, Predetermined Snippets, and Theme Snippets.

Random-shaped Snippets

Many designs can be created entirely with random snippets; a perfect example is the *San Juan Sunset* on page 65. To start, I suggest you just begin snipping fabric to find out which shape or shapes feel the most natural for you to cut. I find that cutting a curvy triangular shape comes natural to me. If you find yourself consistently making similar shapes and would like to change, try turning your wrist in different directions as you cut. Make long thin snippets, or oval snippets. Play with the shapes to see how they affect the look of the design. Move the snippets around

Random snippets

Wild Dolphins II by Cindy Walter, 41″ x 48″. I enjoy reproducing my framed projects into quilts. This quilt was inspired by *The Wild Dolphins* on page 63.

or discard them if they're not "working" for you. Until you fuse the pieces, you have the freedom to play and move the snippets around. When cutting snippets, hold the fabric just above the project with the scissors touching the foundation. This way, the snippets land glue side down as they drop where you want to place them on the project. Use the tip portion of the scissors so the snippets release easily. Tweezers come in handy for moving tiny pieces.

Forces of Conflict by Beverly Colson, 21" x 15". This project demonstrates the use of whole pieces of fabric for the background (panel background) and oval-shaped snippets for the clouds. The scene is highlighted with an appliqued wolf and lightening drawn with fabric paint.

Predetermined Snippets

At times you will want to cut fabric into predetermined (planned) shapes. This is easy to do; you can freely cut shapes without drawing a pattern. In other words, if you need a circle, cut the circle freehanded. If the circle is not completely round, don't worry; I think it is

Image is drawn on the web paper liner.

Web is pre-fused to the fabric.

Pre-fused fabric is cut along the lines and the web paper liner is removed.

Fabric image is flipped and fused onto the background fabric.

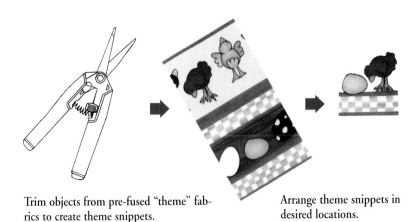

Trim objects from pre-fused "theme" fabrics to create theme snippets.

Arrange theme snippets in desired locations.

better and adds character to the project. *The Kiss*, page 54, is a perfect example of planned shapes.

Another example of a predetermined snippet shape is the wolf in *Forces of Conflict,* at left. In this case, it is actually a form of fusible applique because the artist drew the wolf on the web's paper liner and then adhered the web to the fabric. She then cut the wolf out along the pencil lines and fused it onto the background. I've illustrated this form of applique for you above.

Notice in the illustrations that when you draw or trace a design onto the web paper liner, the end result is a mirror image. Since the drawn image is fused to the wrong side of the fabric, when the fabric is flipped over, the image turns out opposite of how it was drawn.

Theme Snippets

Theme snippets are cut from pre-fused theme fabrics. Cut around the different objects from the pre-fused fabric that you want to include in a Snippet Art project.

Combining Snippet Shapes

If you browse through the Gallery, you'll notice that many of the projects use a combination of snippet shapes. *The Kiss,* page 54, is a wonderful example of combining snippet shapes and panels. *Tranquil Twilight,* page 52, is another example of combining random snippets and predetermined (planned) snippets.

Using an object silhouette is also helpful when creating design elements made with random shaped snippets. To create the dolphins featured in *Wild Dolphins II,* page 36, I first drew the outline of the dolphin shapes on the web paper liner. (I had to remember to draw the dolphins backwards so that when they were flipped over they faced the direction I wanted.) Next, I fused the web to white muslin. Before peeling the paper liner, I cut the dolphins out along the pencil lines and removed the paper. I fused the muslin dolphins onto the snippet background where I wanted them located. Doing this gave me a clear defined outline to work with for the dolphin's snippet placement. Adding an extra fabric layer gave the dolphins a three-dimensional appearance, and also prevented any of the teal background from showing through the lighter colored snippets.

Cutting

Determine which design element to work on first. Remember to start with the element that is farthest away and follow the

The large dolphin-shaped (predetermined) silhouette is fused to the blue background snippets. It will serve as a guide to the placement of the lighter dolphin snippets, and will make the dolphin stand out.

When cutting snippets, hold the fabric just above your project with the scissors touching the foundation. This way, the snippets land glue side down as they drop onto the project.

To cover large areas, start with large-sized snippets.

Next, add layers of medium-sized snippets.

Finally, add a sprinkling of small, delicate snippets.

depth order. Remove the web's paper liner from the first piece of fabric. Hold the fabric, right side up, just above where you want the snippets to fall and begin cutting. The bottom blade of your scissors should touch the foundation. By cutting just above the foundation, you can cause most of the snippets to fall just about where you want them. The pieces can be moved around, but random placement works for most designs. When cutting, use the tip portion of the blade so the snippets easily fall away from the scissors.

Choose the snippet shape and size that best suits your design. To get a jump start you can begin with a bottom layer of larger snippets. These can be as large as two or three inches in diameter. This is how I usually start building layers of color. The large snippets cover large areas quickly. Add layers of medium sized snippets and finish up with a layer of small snippets on top. This makes it appear that you did more work than you did. Parts of the bottom snippet layer peek out, showing color between the upper, smaller snippets. Many of the projects with large areas of snippets use this technique.

Be patient, the first few minutes of cutting snippets may seem awkward; once the design starts to take shape, you will become more comfortable and excited about continuing. I find the first snippets the hardest and the last snippets the easiest. Get started now. Cut the first layer of snippets; fuse if necessary. *Keep cutting.* Many students cut one or two snippets and then agonize over whether they are the correct shape. You will drive yourself crazy this way. Instead, cut a large number of snippets before you start to analyze. You cannot seriously evaluate the picture until you are well into the cutting and fusing process.

Setting Snippets

Fusing, or ironing, permanently adheres pre-fused snippets and panels to the foundation. Traditional web is fused in stages, after every two or three layers of snippets are added. With Steam-A-Seam 2, you can permanently fuse once, after all the layers are in place. One advantage of using Steam-A-Seam 2 is that the fabric pieces adhere with pressure and can be repositioned until ironed.

Try to avoid using thin and thick fabrics in the same areas of the project. They may require different ironing times. Also, dark colors may show through thin or white fabrics layered over them. If this happens, add more layers of the lighter snippets to block out the darker color.

As you iron, pick the iron up and set it down on the next section. *Do not slide the iron across the snippets.* This can disturb the snippets and cause them to move. Occasionally check the iron plate to be sure that there are no snippets sticking to it.

Work in Stages

If you are using Steam-A-Seam 2 fusible web, you do not have to set your project in stages; set once at the end. If you are using traditional web, there are several reasons to set the snippets in stages. If the snippets are more than a few layers thick, the heat does not penetrate through to the bottom layer of snippets. When this happens the snippets will not adhere securely to each other or to the foundation. Fusing snippets in layers prevents them from accidentally being scattered. You also get a better perspective of the design development when the pieces are ironed flat. As the snippets are set, the colors start to blend and you can tell if more snippets of any color are needed.

Continue the cutting process until satisfied with the outcome. Periodically, step back about ten feet and look at the project. At this distance the fabric colors blend and give you an overall view of how the picture is developing. Add each design element following the depth order until all the components are created and fused to the base.

Setting Snippets

Before ironing, look closely and make sure all snippets are glue side down.

For traditional web, iron according to the instructions on the web's package to permanently fuse the snippets to the foundation as each layer is completed.

For Steam-A-Seam 2, use hand pressure to temporarily set snippets in place. Iron according to the instructions on the web's package when ready to permanently fuse the snippets to the foundation.

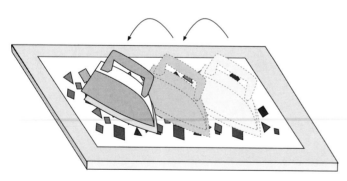

As you iron, pick the iron up and set it down on the next section. Do not *slide* the iron across the snippets.

Troubleshooting

Problem: Snippets are not sticking.

Solution: If you have a problem with a snippet or a section of snippets not sticking to the foundation, check the wrong side of the fabric. Can you see the coating of glue? If so, the snippets need more heat. Touch the area with an iron for a few more seconds. On the other hand, if the glue is no longer visible, it has melted into the fabric. You can do one of following:

• Pull the snippet, or section, off and start over with new snippets.

• Cover the snippet, or section, with additional snippets to "trap" them in place.

• Put a dab of fabric glue under the snippet, or section, to adhere it in place. The glue dries clear and won't show. If you have already framed the project, I suggest this method.

Tips: To avoid this problem, become more familiar with your fusible web brand. Carefully reread the package instructions. Experiment with the web on some scrap fabric. You may need to make adjustments to the heating time or turn down temperature on your iron.

Recap

Use sharp, comfortable scissors to cut the snippets. Snippets can be cut any shape or size. Remember to work in depth order when creating the design elements. Just get started, and don't evaluate your work until you have cut many layers of snippets and the image is taking form. Continue cutting layers of snippets and fusing as necessary.

"Setting" Snippets

For traditional web, use heat to permanently fuse snippets to the foundation as each layer is completed.

For Steam-A-Seam 2, use light hand pressure to set snippets in place. Iron when ready to permanently fuse them to the foundation. Fuse the project all at once when the entire design is complete.

Troubleshooting

Problem: There is paper left on the back of your snippets.

Solutions: Everyone makes this mistake at least once. You have two choices:

✓ Peel the paper off each snippet. This is tedious, but may prove worthwhile for large snippets or specialty fabrics.

✓ Dump these snippets in the trash and pre-fuse a new piece of fabric. This is my choice!

STEP 11 *Review the Project*

Troubleshooting

Problem: Mistakes or areas you are not pleased with.

Solution: As you work, or later during the review, you can correct mistakes or change areas that you find disappointing. It is possible to pull snippets off while they are still warm, but this is messy. The easiest way to make a change is to cover the area with a fresh layer of snippets.

Tip: Using Steam-A-Seam 2 can help avoid the problem. Since the web is pressure sensitive, the snippets stick with the pressure of your hand. You iron the project just once, after reviewing and making any necessary changes.

Once you feel the project is complete, leave it for several hours or days. Come back later for a final review. Are you happy with the colors, shapes, and mood of the picture? Ask your friends. What do they see? You can change areas you are unhappy with or fix mistakes. See the Troubleshooting hints on this page. You can add more snippets to the project at any time. After it cools, the web glue re-solidifies and you are able to re-iron it. You can even add snippets after the project is quilted or framed. I added cherry colored leaves to my *Autumn Trees,* below, one year after it was originally "finished." I had quilted this project so I just ironed on the additional snippets. To add to framed projects, I recommend using fabric glue. I would not suggest "touching up" an expensively framed project with a hot iron.

If you are done snipping and cutting, review your work again. Start considering what embellishments to add, and how to frame or quilt the project. Don't trim away the extra base fabric until you are ready to add borders, or until you know how much excess fabric is needed for the framing process.

Recap

Step back from your project and take a long look. Are you happy with the design? Is there anything to change? Anything to add? Remember, you can add to the project at any time in the future, but it may not be as easy to do as it is now.

Autumn Trees by Cindy Walter, 29 ″ x 21 ″. The bright cherry red leaves in this piece were added one year after I "finished" the project!

STEP 12 *Embellish*

Embellishing is optional, but what fun! Embellishments of any nature can be used to enhance Snippet designs. Glue dried flowers to the tops of snippet flowers in a garden. Use lace for curtains or real buttons down the front of a dress. Place twigs on tree trunks for branches. Use fabric pens and fabric paints for adding delicate details, or spray glitter onto blue fabric to create glistening water. Think about all the different types of embellishments you could use to adorn your design.

Considerations

The variety of embellishments are endless. They can be glued, sewn, or sprayed onto projects. Most often, I use fabric glue. There are many brands on the market that are easy to apply and that dry clear. A hot glue gun is also a handy tool. Using glue, you can attach nearly any item to your project. Unique fabrics, fibers, threads, and yarns add texture to a project. Some thought needs to be taken when embellishing projects that will be framed and covered with glass. Make sure the embellishments do not protrude too far from the surface. The glass could compress them into the project.

Remember September by Mary Beth Mills, 29" x 19".

Examples

Many of the projects pictured in this book have added embellishments. The shading on the bridge in *Remember September*, above right, is done with fabric pens. Fabric paint is used to outline the wolf and lightning in *Forces of Conflict*, page 37. The result is stunning.

Wheat Country, at right, has an assortment of embellishments. Strips of gold velvet add texture and create realistic furrows in the fields. Fancy embroidery stitches simulate grass and weeds near the bottom of the piece. Beautiful beads and threads also decorate this project, which is made entirely from theme fabrics.

Wheat Country by Mary Ann Nickell, 26" x 21".

Renoir's Little Girl in the Garden, page 15, has some interesting embellishments. The artist used an iron-on transfer for the girl's beautiful facial features. She also used doll hair and a real satin ribbon for the hair bow. Interesting items were also added to *Ashley's Ecstasy*, page 67. Beads, lace, and shiny threads cover the dress.

Another example of unique embellishing can be found in *Rooster*, page 46. The artist glued on actual rooster feathers for the tail and wrapped chicken wire around the frame.

1960s Modern Art, at left, was inspired by a painting from the late '60s. Flowers, leaves, and stems cover the black foundation. The centers of the daffodils are gold buttons. The bees are sewn-on appliqués. The butterfly in the top right corner is three-dimensional: the top wing is lined and stands up, allowing the butterfly to fly into the picture. In *Floral Refractions,* below, velour and a variety of other fabrics add texture. The curtain hangs from a tiny rod. What a beautiful bouquet!

Recap

Would an embellishment enhance your picture? There are many kinds. They can be ironed, glued, drawn, painted, or sewn on. Have fun searching for and creating the finishing touches for your project.

1960s Modern Art by Patricia Clay, 27" x 30".

Floral Refractions by Melissa Jane Dawson, 52" x 30".

STEP 13 *Finish the Project*

Now is the time to decide if you should frame your project or finish it as a quilt. There are several factors that may help you with this decision.

First, what is the mood of the project? Is it homespun and folksy, or is it a "stately" piece of artwork? As an example, the darling *Summertime Flowers*, at right, speaks out and says, "Quilt me, I am folksy and fun." On the other hand, I felt that *Water Lilies at Giverny*, below right, should be framed in a formal way.

The second factor to consider is how your project will be used. Will it hang in a living room (framed), or in the guest bedroom (quilted)? How does the project present itself in different locations?

Summertime Flowers by Laura Van Der Vliet, 25" x 21".

Finally, what is the easiest for you? If you are a quilter, you probably have backing fabric and batting at home. If this is the case, then you may find quilting the project is the easiest and fastest way to finish your project. If you do not have quilting supplies, it may be easier for you to drop the project off at a frame shop and pick it up later, ready to be hung in your home.

Regardless of how you finish the project, you need to sign and date it! Remember, this is a piece of art, and artists should always sign their work. There are may ways to do this. I use a fabric pen to sign my initials and the year in one of the bottom corners. You may want to use a label on the back. I love to read interesting facts about a quilt or picture— what inspired the artist, where the fabrics came from, and who it was made for are a few details you can include.

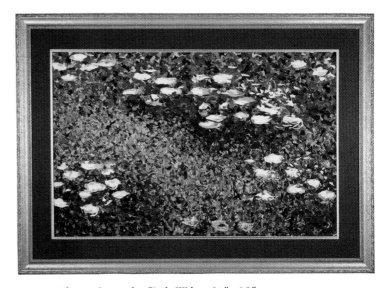

Water Lilies at Giverny by Cindy Walter, 51" x 36".

Framing

Keep in mind that if you choose to frame your art work, the mat and frame are also important parts of the design. Selecting a mat and frame that complement your work will make the overall project outstanding. It also adds a finishing touch to the artwork. I suggest using glass or plexiglass to prevent dust from collecting on your project. Visit a local frame shop to browse the stock and get framing ideas.

There are three options for framing a Snippet Art work: professional framing, doing it yourself at a framing shop, or buying pre-made materials and framing the project at home.

Option 1—Professional Framing

Having a professional framer do the job is more expensive, but the results look professional. This option allows a project to be any finished size. Do not trim away the extra foundation fabric until you have checked with the framer. To stabilize the project, a professional framer may decide to stretch the project around wood bars (like a painter's canvas). Therefore, the framer will need the extra fabric. I worked too closely to the edges of the foundation when creating *Water Lilies at Giverny*. I had to sew 4″ borders of white muslin around the project so that the framer had enough fabric to stretch around the wood bars.

I like taking my work to a professional framer. They do quality work and offer great advice. There are so many choices when it comes to mats and frames. Mats come in a huge variety of colors. Should I use one or two mats, or maybe none at all? What type of material should I select for the frame: wood, plastic, or metal? What about color and thickness? Help! Professional framers can usually help you narrow down the choices.

Rooster by Mary Ann Nickell, 18 ″ x 21 ″. Mary Ann went beyond the framing options listed here and completely customized her frame. The wood frame is painted bright red and is wrapped with chicken wire to make her rooster feel right at home.

Option 2—Self-Framing Shops

Going to a "do-it-yourself" frame shop and custom framing your Snippet Art project is a great in-between option. It can keep the framing costs down, but places fewer restrictions on the project size than using pre-made frames. Talk with the employees at the shop; they can offer you good advice. To stabilize your project, I suggest that you use mounting or foam board instead of stretching bars. Trim the foundation fabric so it does not hang over the edges of the board.

Option 3—Pre-Made Frames

The third option is the least expensive, but does restrict the size of the project. You can frame the project quickly and simply at home, but there are fewer choices in color and quality of the materials. To frame the project yourself, buy a standard-sized mounting board, mat, and frame. There is a wider variety of small and medium sized pre-made frames than larger sizes. Plan the project size accordingly. The following section goes over how to frame the project using pre-made frames.

To frame your project yourself:

You will need a self-adhesive mounting board, a mat, and a frame in compatible sizes. You will also require the hardware to hang the frame. Follow this procedure to assemble and frame a Snippet Art project.

1. Place the mat on top of the picture to determine what part of the picture should show through the mat opening. Place small pieces of masking tape at each edge of the mat opening. These guide marks will be used for centering the design on the mounting board. (See illustration A.)

2. Using the masking tape as a guide, trim the foundation fabric 1½″ from the outside edges of the masking tape guides. (See illustration B.)

3. Peel the paper off the mounting board exposing the sticky adhesive surface. Move the Snippet Art into position on top of the mounting board. Center the project and then stretch it toward the edges. Press down firmly to attach it to the board. (See illustration C.)

4. Place the mat on top of the picture and mounting board. Place the frame on top of the mat. (See illustration D.)

5. Carefully turn the project over and have the back of the frame toward you. Bend the tabs over the edge of the project layers or insert the clamps. This holds everything in place.

    Note Some frames do not come with any means of holding the project layers in place. Packages of glazer points or clamps can be purchased at framing stores.

6. Usually, a hook for hanging the frame is included. Attach the hanger to the upper edge of the frame on the back side.

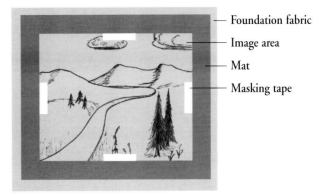

A) Use mat and masking tape to mark image area.

— Foundation fabric
— Image area
— Mat
— Masking tape

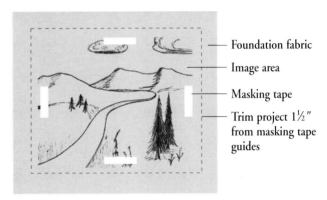

B) Trim foundation fabric 1½″ from the tape guides.

— Foundation fabric
— Image area
— Masking tape
— Trim project 1½″ from masking tape guides

C) Center project on mounting board.

— Mounting board
— Trimmed project

D) Cover mounting board and project with mat and frame.

— Project
— Mat
— Frame

A) Measure the longest sides of the project.

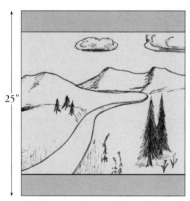

B) Cut two borders to this length and the desired width. Sew them on.

C) Measure the remaining sides of the project, including borders.

D) Cut two borders to this length and the desired width. Sew them on.

Quilting

These items are needed to quilt your Snippet project: borders (optional), batting, backing and binding fabric, sewing machine, thread, darning foot, and a topstitch needle (90/14). (See "Suggested Reading," page 94, for a list of books that cover each of these topics in detail.)

Borders

Borders are another wonderful way to "frame" Snippet projects. Select the border fabric by spreading a bolt of fabric open and laying the project in the center of the fabric. Does the fabric enhance the project? Not all projects need a border. The project size and the desired width of the borders determine the amount of fabric you need.

To measure, cut, and sew borders:

1. Trim away any excess foundation, leaving ¼″ seam allowances to sew on the borders.

2. Decide how wide to make the border pieces. There is no strict rule on how wide to make borders.

3. As an example, let's take a project that is 20″ x 24″ with 3″ wide border pieces. Measure the longest side of the project. The first two borders to be sewn on are this length, 24″, by 3″ wide. (See illustration A.)

4. Cut the first two borders and sew them to the longest sides of the quilt top using ¼″ seam allowances. (See illustration B.)

5. Measure the remaining two sides, including the width of both borders. The remaining two borders are this length, 25″, by 3″ wide. (See illustration C.)

6. Cut the remaining two borders and sew them on using a ¼″ seam allowance. (See illustration D.)

Batting

For projects that I hand quilt, I prefer a thin cotton or polyester batting. For machine quilting I like Warm & Natural® cotton batting. Cut the batting 6″ longer and wider than the size of the quilt top.

Backing

The backing fabric can be a plain cotton muslin or a print fabric that coordinates with the colors or design theme of the top. I pre-wash my backing fabric and then steam iron it to remove any wrinkles. Cut the backing piece the same size as the batting. If the project is larger than the width of the backing fabric, sew two widths of the backing fabric together. Center the seam on the back of the quilt.

The "Quilt Sandwich"

The quilt layers are stacked in a "quilt sandwich" and then basted together to keep them from shifting as the quilting is done.

To prepare the layers of a quilt for quilting:

1. Lay the backing, right side down, on a table or hard floor (not carpet). Tape the sides to hold the backing flat and taut.

2. Next, lay the batting over the backing. Smooth it out so there are no wrinkles or lumps.

3. Center the Snippet quilt top, right side up, on top of the batting.

4. Baste the layers together using your favorite basting method. I prefer safety pin basting. Unlike standard quilting, Snippet Art projects need a minimal amount of basting. It is best to baste through the thinnest layers of snippets, or through areas of exposed foundation.

Free-motion quilting

This is my favorite method of quilting my Snippet projects. I suggest that you practice on a small quilt "sandwich."

Quilting Designs and Quilting

Snippet projects consist of many layers of fabric and web glue and, therefore, machine quilting is the easiest way to quilt them. You can hand quilt in the exposed foundation areas.

Snippet Art is a technique that allows you to express your inner artistic soul. Let your quilting express the movement of the design; this is called free-motion quilting. Water could be quilted with long wavy lines. A building could be quilted with straight lines. Some quilters prefer very little quilting, while others like to quilt the entire surface.

Complete the quilting, trim off the excess batting and backing, and remove the basting.

In *Mt. Rainier,* by Cindy Walter, the sky area is machine quilted with cloud shapes.

Binding

Now the binding can be added to finish the edges of the quilt. I like to treat the binding as a final border, or the final color to frame the quilt. If you are unfamiliar with binding techniques, there are many quilting reference books that have thorough instructions for calculating and adding the binding to a quilt. Several of these books are listed in the Suggested Reading list, page 94.

Recap

Decide whether to quilt or frame your project. If you plan to frame, stop by your local frame or craft store and get some advice. If you want to quilt the project and have never quilted before, I suggest that you take a quilting class at your local quilt store. You can also refer to one of the quilting books found on the Suggested Reading list for more information about quilting and finishing the edges.

The exposed foundation of Cindy Walter's *Festive Wreath* is hand quilted in a grid pattern.

14 *Clean Up*

Wow, you're done! But wait, there are a few more things to go over. Don't throw those leftover pre-fused fabric scraps away—keep them for future projects, or let the kids have fun creating their own work of art.

Storing Leftover Fabric

Store unused pieces of fabric pre-fused with traditional web flat, with a light weight (book) placed on top. This prevents the fabric from curling or folding. If the fabric does curl, iron it flat by using a piece of web liner to cover the exposed glue surface. Iron for just one second. Remember, the waxed side of the paper covers the glue; do not touch the wax or glue with the iron. If the fabric is not flat, the snippets will curl as you cut them. This makes it difficult to iron them.

If you use Steam-A-Seam 2, the unused pieces of pre-fused fabric can be stored with the web still attached. Cover the exposed web with a layer of the paper liner for storing. A great feature of this product is that the web layer can be peeled off the fabric. The fabric and the web can then be used for other projects. If you remove Steam-A-Seam 2 web from the fabric, place it back on the protective paper liner.

I sort my leftover pre-fused fabric by color. This makes it easy to collect the colors I need for the fabric palette when I start a new Snippet Art project.

Water World by Robert Kenneth Henry, 25 ″ x 32 ″. This piece was created by Marilyn Doheny-Smith's young neighbor, using scraps from *Perennial Pleasures*.

Storing Unused Web

Store unused web flat or rolled, but not folded. The glue does not coat the fabric evenly where there are creases. Several people have mentioned to me that they have had trouble with "old" web stored for a year or more. I have not experienced this myself, but my advice to you is to buy only the amount of web that you might use up in a few months.

Cleaning Your Iron

The final stage is to clean your iron. I recommend using Dritz Iron-Off®. It works very well in removing any traces of "gunk." (Although, I find that if I leave the "gunk" on my iron, no one in my family asks me to iron their clothes!)

Recap

Store your unused pre-fused fabric scraps flat. Remember to clean your iron when you finish so you are ready to start a new project. If it becomes necessary to wash your project, keep it as flat as possible, and use cool water and mild soap.

Snippet Art Care

Protect your project from wear and tear by hanging it on a wall.

If your artwork has been framed behind glass or plexi–glass, it should stay protected from dust.

If your Snippet quilt becomes dusty or dirty, wash it by laying it flat in the bathtub. Use cool water and mild soap. Dry flat.

GALLERY

Water Lilies at Giverny
by Cindy Walter
• 51″ x 36″
• Snippet Background
• Framed

This project was a lesson in color. At first glance, the background in Monet's original painting appears purple and green. Upon closer examination, many, many more colors become apparent. This was not a difficult design, but it took several weeks to gather all the fabrics.

Tranquil Twilight
by Cindy Walter
• 26″ x 20″
• Snippet Background
• Framed

A special thanks to Hoffman Fabrics for providing the fabric for this picture. The fabric was so stunning that I was instantly inspired to create this beautiful sunset.

Girl Before a Mirror
by Cindy Walter

• 20 " x 24 "
• Panel Background
• Framed

Pablo Picasso inspired my first attempt at abstract design with the Snippet Art technique. All the snippets are planned, predetermined shapes. A special thank you to Alaska Dyeworks for providing the fabrics for this work.

Sunburst
by Sean Porterfield

• 15 " x 13 "
• Exposed Foundation
• Framed

Sean attended Two Rivers Alternative High School in North Bend, Washington, where I shared Snippet Art with students. All the kids were successful with the technique, but Sean excelled. His design won a blue ribbon in the county-wide *Hearts for the Arts* competition.

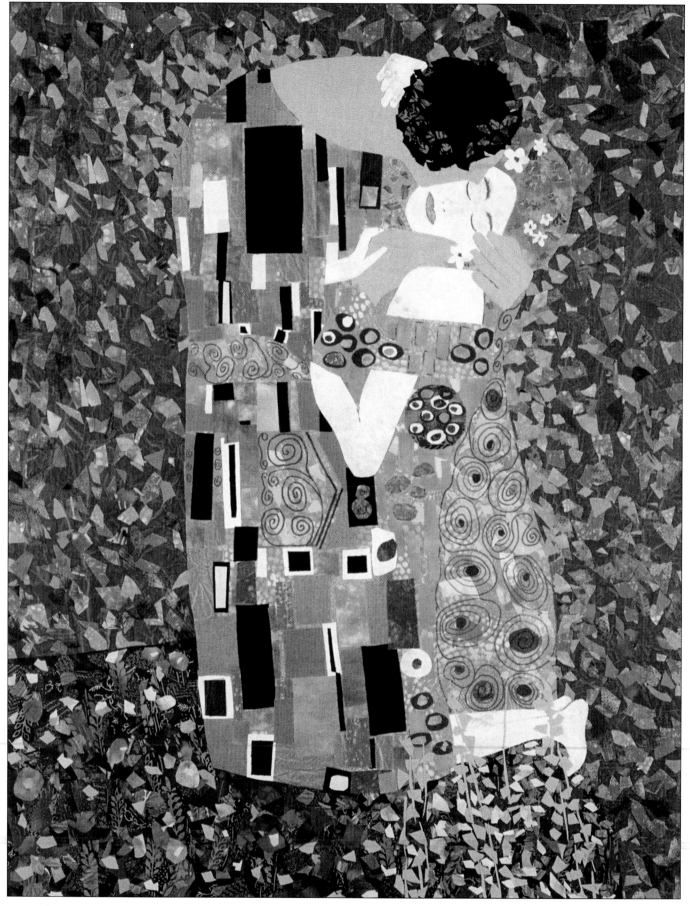

The Kiss
by Cindy Walter

54

- 26" x 31"
- Snippet Background
- Framed

The passion in Klimt's paintings inspired me to create *The Kiss* using the Snippet technique. I drew details on the woman's face and dress with fabric pens.

The Kiss II
by Cindy Walter

• 40″ x 47″

I have taught quilting for over a decade, so I enjoy reproducing my framed projects into quilts. This quilt was inspired by *The Kiss*.

The Three Goddesses
by Elizabeth Fontanilla
- 28″ x 42″
- Panel Background
- Framed

Elizabeth, a Hawaiian artist, typically captures the beauty of the islands in oils or watercolors. Hawaiian folklore inspired this picture. Elizabeth drew the faces with fabric pens and added touches of gold and silver with metallic ink. She was inspired to write this poem about the goddesses.

The Three Goddesses

From the realms of mist and rain
Lay crystal mantled queen
Poliahu's cold domain
Snow capped Mauna Kea

Molten lava, thundering earth
Smoke and ash, flame and fire
Destruction and again, rebirth
Pele's Kilauea

Many a mortal man's cold grave
Home of dolphin and of whale
Rules she there beneath the wave
Na-maka-o-kaha'i

Perennial Pleasures
by Marilyn Doheny-Smith

- 22" x 36"
- Exposed Foundation
- Quilted

Marilyn loves flowers and is giving this quilt to her friend, Mary Rucker, so that she will have a beautiful bouquet to cheer her in the wintertime.

Iris
by Linda Lacy

- 16" x 19"
- Exposed Foundation
- Framed

Linda cut predetermined shapes to create her regal iris.

57

Behind the Picket Fence
by Sharon Gordon

- 24″ x 20″
- Exposed Foundation
- Framed

Delicate snippets of pre-determined shapes form the pink flower petals. Kittens cut from theme fabric add a whimsical note.

Hibiscus
by Diana Morrison

- 20″ x 18″
- Exposed Foundation
- Framed

Diana found her inspiration on a greeting card. Shades Hand Dyed Textiles provided the beautiful fabrics, which create a wonderful effect of sunlight playing on petals and leaves.

Covered Bridge of Madison County
by Lynda Bass
- 18″ x 14″
- Panel and Snippet Background
- Framed

Lynda has always loved covered bridges.

Gone But Not Forgotten
by Michele LeDoux Sakurai
- 14″ x 18″
- Exposed Foundation
- Framed

Michele made this quilt in memory of her husband's grandfather, as a reflection of his continuing journey. The foundation is a single piece of fabric that shades from blue to black. Perfect fabric choices make this a spectacular portrait.

Cottonwoods Along the Rio Grande by Linda Lacy
- 30" x 19"
- Exposed Foundation
- Framed

Linda is from New Mexico and was inspired to make a Snippet Art design of cottonwoods remembered from her childhood. The elongated snippets in the river create the effect of moving water. Gold highlights make this a striking picture.

Wheat Country by Mary Ann Nickell
- 26" x 21"
- Panel Background
- Framed

Sky, fields, and barn are cut from theme fabrics. Strips of velour are used to create furrows in the fields. Elaborate embellishments including embroidery and beads adorn the entire picture, adding texture and interest.

60

Tea House
by Diane Ross

- 26″ x 28″
- Snippet Background
- Framed

Gardening, especially Japanese style gardening, is close to this artist's heart. Here she has created a fabric garden that showcases fall's beauty. The design is inspired by a photograph taken by Sam Abell.

Wagon Wheel Memories
by Lynda Bass
• 11″ x 10″
• Snippet Background
• Framed

Lynda cut leaves and flowers from theme fabrics to adorn this charming wagon wheel.

Garden Door
by Donna Bridgeman
• 22″ x 24″
• Panel Background
• Framed

This lovely garden scene uses a combination of snippet shapes. The foundation fabric was covered with panels of purple, red, and green. Then Donna laid snippets of pre-determined shapes over them for the shadows, leaves, and flowers.

Wild Dolphins
by Cindy Walter
- 25″ x 32″
- Snippet Background
- Framed

This design was inspired by friends recalling their exciting adventure swimming with wild dolphins in Hawaii. The outline of each dolphin was drawn on the paper side of the fusible web, which was then fused to muslin. The muslin was cut on the lines and fused to the snippet background. Elongated snippets on the dolphin bodies create the sense of motion as they glide through the water.

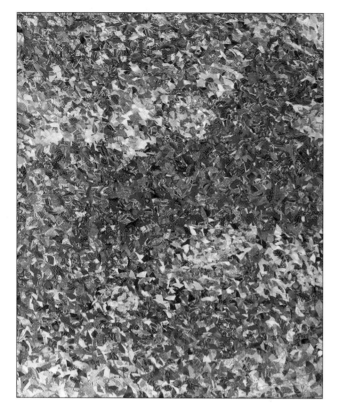

For the Love of Monet by Cindy Schindler
- 23" x 26"
- Snippet Background
- Quilted

Snippets cut from a variety fabrics create a beautiful impressionistic version of Monet's lily pond.

Watercolor Heart by Vickie McKenney
- 21" x 24" • Snippet Background • Quilted

Vickie owns the wonderful Calico Basket quilting store in Edmonds, Washington. Her lovely heart, made of floral fabrics, was inspired by the book *Watercolor Quilts,* by Pat Maixner Magaret and Donna Ingram Slusser.

Lilacs by Patricia Thompson
- 20" x 28" • Exposed Foundation • Framed

This piece was inspired by the artworks of Manet. After fusing the stem snippets in the vase, Patricia added gray fabric, silver lamé, and white netting to simulate shimmering water. Small black fabric accents were added to the stems and vase as highlights.

San Juan Sunset
by Linda Gould
• 29" x 23"
• Snippet Background
• Framed

The view from the artist's San Juan Island property inspired this design. Notice how Linda used yellow snippets to simulate the sun's reflection in the golden waters.

Tropical Sunset
by Lynda Bass
• 17" x 23"
• Snippet Background
• Framed

The purple snippets used for the clouds create a stunning effect over the bright yellow and orange sunset. The palm trees are covered with black netting, giving them a soft, shadowy look.

Mt. Rainier
by Cindy Walter
• 25″ x 20″
• Exposed Foundation
• Quilted

This design was inspired by beautiful Mt. Rainier in Washington. It was my second Snippet project, made only a week after I created the technique.

The Mission
by Michelle Winter
• 24″ x 20″
• Exposed Foundation
• Quilted

A base of white fabric creates the mission shape. The building was drawn on the paper side of the fusible web. The stone relief of the monk was drawn in with fabric pen.

Ashley's Ecstasy
by Cindy McNutt-Kaestner
• *38" x 53"*
• Snippet Background
• Quilted

Cindy photographed her daughter, Ashley, and blew the photo up to life size on a copy machine. She used this as a pattern and traced it onto the paper liner of her fusible webbing. She cut the pattern pieces apart and fused them to the fabrics. These pieces served as a base on which the design was created. The portrait is beautifully machine quilted using several decorative threads.

PART III

Step-by-Step Projects

PROJECT 1

Festive Wreath

Snippet Sensations is remarkably versatile. Using the directions for the Festive Wreath, you can make a Christmas Wreath wall hanging or, by changing the colors in the fabric palette, you can assemble a wreath to fit any seasonal theme. Substitute autumn fabrics, tiny pine cones, and miniature Indian corn cobs for a colorful Thanksgiving wall hanging. I guarantee that making a wreath with the Snippet technique will be fun and enjoyable.

Background Style:
Exposed Foundation

This project uses an Exposed Foundation background style. Reflect on your choice of fabric for the foundation, as it is part of the design. I chose an unadorned white fabric to let the wreath and bow become the dominant design elements.

Project Supply List

- **Foundation Fabric:** 1 yard, or a piece of fabric cut to 22″ x 26″
- **Palette Fabrics:** 6 shades red (⅟₁₆ yard total) 6 shades green (⅟₁₆ yard total) 4 shades blue (scraps)
  2 shades gold (scraps) 2 shades yellow (scraps) 2 shades peach (scraps)
- **Backing Fabric:** 1 yard, or a piece of fabric cut to 24″ x 28″
- **Binding Fabric:** ¼ yard (I used red for my binding)
- **Batting:** Piece cut to 24″ x 28″
- **Fusible Web:** 2 yards
- **Embellishments:** Gold bow (2 yards of 2″ wide wire-edged ribbon), ornaments, other embellishments
- **Scissors**
- **Ironing supplies:** Iron and ironing board or cardboard ironing surface
- **General quilting supplies**

Project Instructions

Each of the following steps is discussed in greater detail in the previous section. Any time you need a review, turn back to the corresponding step in Part II.

1 *Choose a Design*

The inspiration for this design came from a greeting card by Rita Yeasting. The basic shape and simple background make it a great "starter" project. The many colors used in the wreath also make it a fun and endlessly variable project. (See pages 75–77 for some exciting examples.)

2 *Select a Background Style*

This project is well suited for an Exposed Foundation background. A solid color fabric, a subdued print, or any fabric that enhances the design would work well for the foundation. Steam iron the fabric. Cut the foundation 22˝ x 26˝.

3 *Collect Palette Fabrics*

Use the list of palette fabrics in the Supply List to gather the fabric colors. You can use more or fewer colors for your project. For future projects you can completely change the color scheme to create wreaths with other themes.

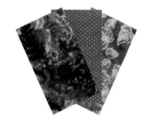

4 *Select Fusible Web*

Choose a fusible web. Read the package directions carefully. I prefer Steam-A-Seam 2.

5 *Gather Ironing Equipment*

Gather your ironing supplies. You need a steam iron and an ironing surface. Take precautions to protect the iron and ironing surface.

6 *Pre-Fuse Palette Fabrics*

Iron the palette fabrics with a hot steam iron to remove wrinkles and to preshrink. Pre-fuse the web to the back of the fabrics, following the instructions included with the web. Peel off the paper liner before cutting any snippets!

> ### *Pre-Fusing*
>
> ***For traditional web products,*** such as Aleene's, Heat N Bond, and Wonder-Under, use the heat of an iron to pre-fuse the fabrics.
>
> ***For Steam-A-Seam 2,*** use the pressure of your hand to pre-fuse the fabrics.

7 Trim Palette Fabrics

Clean up the pre-fused fabric by trimming away frayed edges, fabric areas without glue, or excess web hanging over the fabric edges.

8 Determine Depth Order

The foundation fabric (1) is the background for the project. It is the element farthest away in depth. Next in depth order is the wreath foliage (2). The closest elements are flowers; the long thin poinsettia snippets, small holly berries, and yellow flower centers (3). This is the order to follow for creating the wreath. Embellishments such as the bow (4) are added later in Step 12.

9 Create the Background

Since the foundation fabric is the background, you are ready to start. Lay the fabric on an ironing board or a large piece of cardboard. Iron with steam to remove all wrinkles. If you would like a guide for snippet placement, lightly draw a circle on the foundation the approximate size of the wreath. This will help you keep the wreath in a circular shape.

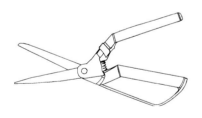

10 Cut and Fuse Snippets

Let's start the wreath. As you cut the layers of snippets, reserve a 3″ square of each fabric. Sometimes a color gets completely buried and you may decide later to add a splash of this color on top.

1. Start with a 4″ x 6″ piece of dark green fabric. Hold the fabric just above the foundation. Cut large random snippets around the entire wreath. Do the same for the remaining greens, the reds and the golds. As you cut, move the fabric so that the snippets form the wreath's general shape. Starting with larger snippets gives you a "jump start" on the wreath. (See "Project In Progress" on page 72.)

2. Once you have a rough circle formed with a layer of the larger snippets, make sure that all the snippets are glue side down. Set them in place if using traditional web.

3. You are now ready for the next snippet layers. Taking a 4″ x 6″ piece of each green, cut medium-sized snippets around the entire wreath. Cut one color of green at a time. Do the same with the light and medium shades of the reds and golds. Set these layers of snippets if using traditional web.

4. Add medium-sized snippets of dark reds and peaches in three or four concentrated areas on the wreath. These snippets will determine the flower areas.

"Setting" Snippets

For traditional web, use heat to permanently fuse snippets to the foundation as each layer is completed.

For Steam-A-Seam 2, use light hand pressure to set snippets in place. Iron when ready to permanently fuse them to the foundation. Fuse the project all at once when the entire design is complete.

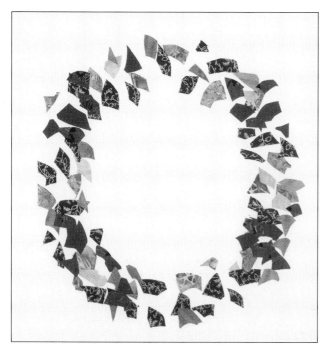

Begin with large snippets in various shades of green, red, and gold.

Add a layer of medium size snippets of green, red, and gold. Add concentrated areas of dark reds and peaches at flower areas and sprinkles of blues and golds around the wreath.

Build up the flowers with long, thin strips of lighter shades of red. Add dots of red for holly berries and bits of yellow for the flower centers.

Review your work and add snippets of various colors as you desire until you feel the wreath is complete.

5. Add sprinkles of the blues and golds around the whole wreath for a touch of accent color.

6. On top of the medium-sized snippets, cut smaller snippets from all the colors until you have added another layer or two. Stop when the wreath looks filled in and full. Set the snippets to the foundation if using traditional web.

7. Build up the flowers. Cut long, thin strips of the lighter reds and place them in a circular pattern over the dark red and peach areas.

8. Cut small red fabric dots for holly berries and small snippets from the yellows for the centers of the flowers.

9. Check that all the snippets are glue side down. Permanently fuse all the layers to the foundation.

11 Review the Project

Stand back about ten feet and review your Snippet project. Check the overall effect. Is there enough color and character? Are the flowers distinguishable? Are there areas that look too thin or undeveloped? Is the wreath shape pleasing to you? Now is the time for those final snippets to fill in areas, or cover over areas, that need changes. For my project, I added additional dabs of each color and more flowers. Fuse the entire project one last time.

I usually let a project rest for a few days and then come back for a final critique. Examine your project with a fresh outlook. Add any additional snippets and fuse them in place. You are now ready to add embellishments and quilt.

12 Embellish

I added eight gold-toned charms and a large ribbon bow. For this project, it is easier to quilt the wreath before adding any embellishments. We'll come back to this later.

At this point, secure any embellishments that you feel won't be in the way while you quilt.

Creative Beginnings carries an amazing assortment of decorative charms, in gold and pewter tones, that can be used to embellish almost anything. See "Supply Sources" on page 93.

13 Finish the Project

The wreath project seemed well suited to being quilted. Since the exposed foundation was bare of any snippets, I could easily hand quilt through the exposed areas. The Suggested Reading list, page 93, lists several books that thoroughly cover the subjects of general quilt construction, hand and machine quilting, and binding.

Borders

I elected not to add any borders to my wreath project. Several of the wreaths created for the "wreath test project" do have borders. Survey the wreath pictures, pages 75–77, for inspiration on borders and quilting designs. You can add borders by following the instructions in Part II, page 47. Remember, though, this will change the finished size of your project and it will require larger backing and batting pieces.

Regardless of whether you add a border, the project needs to be trimmed to the finished size. Cut the foundation to 22" x 26" before adding any desired borders.

Quilting

I decided a simple, diagonal grid quilting design would set off and contrast agreeably with the free-form wreath design. Decide what pattern you want to use to quilt your wreath. Lay the quilt top on a flat, smooth surface and mark the quilting design lines with a quilt marking pen or pencil.

Make a "quilt sandwich" with the backing, batting, and quilt top. Baste the layers together using your preferred method. Quilt the design either by hand or machine.

Binding

Use your preferred binding method to finish the quilt edges.

Back to Embellishments

Tie and make a bow with the ribbon. I made mine with gold, wire-edged ribbon. This way the bow is pliable and holds its shape. Secure the bow and charms to the quilt using fabric glue.

14 Clean Up

Wow! You're finished! Wasn't it fun, fast, and easy? Be sure that your iron is clean. Store the unused pieces of pre-fused fabric in a flat position so that they are ready for your next project. A wreath wall hanging makes a wonderful gift for any occasion—a surprise birthday present for someone special, or a baby theme wall hanging for a new mom.

You probably want to begin your next project tomorrow. Create another wreath wall hanging, try one of the other sample projects, or design a stunning showpiece of your own!

Reinterpreting the Design

The wreath below and the three on the following page were created by my students. Each artist started with Rita Yeasting's wreath design, left, as her inspiration, and then made her own creation using individual expressions of color, form, and embellishment. Each wreath is unique, and all are enchanting!

Holiday Wreath greeting card by Rita Yeasting.

Festive Wreath by Gail Newman, 27" x 27½".

Festive Wreath by Marilyn Doheny-Smith, 38″ x 38″.

Festive Wreath by Nickie Travis, 29″ x 29″.

Festive Wreath by Diane Roubal, 33½″ x 33½″.

Harvest by Cindy Walter. Fall fabrics, dried pinecones, and flowers are combined to make this harvest quilt.

Spring is Here by Cindy Walter. Pastel fabrics, theme fabrics with printed butterflies, and gold charms are combined for this spring quilt.

Christmas Pinks by Cindy Walter. Scraps of cherry, pink, gold, and green fabrics along with a gold bow make this stunning wreath.

2 *Soaring Eagle*

Finished Size: 14" x 11"   Image Size: 9½" x 7½"

This is not a difficult project! I believe you can finish this exciting design in just one afternoon. Two different *Soaring Eagle* finished works are included in this book. I made the framed version pictured above as a Christmas gift. I then created a second eagle to use as a teaching example. It is featured on page 83. The two versions are not exact duplicates, but this is what's so wonderful about the Snippet technique. Even if you decide to repeat a project, it can be different, yet just as outstanding.

Background Style: Panel Background

This project uses a Panel Background style. Several panels of fabric cover the foundation fabric to create a landscape of hills and sky. The eagle is then created with snippets on top of the background. The primary task is to find fabrics that create a stirring background for your eagle to sweep across. This project uses both large and small delicate predetermined snippets. I've included a pattern to use for the base body layer of the eagle, and illustrations of snippet shapes to use when cutting the eagle's feathers.

Project Instructions

Each of the following steps is discussed in greater detail in the previous section. If at any time you need a review, turn back to the corresponding step in Part II.

1 Choose a Design

This design was chosen to show a clear, concise example of Snippet Sensations with a Panel Background. Have fun "trying out" fabrics to use for the background panels that completely cover the foundation fabric. Page 9 shows you what my project looked like before it was framed.

2 Select a Background Style

Since the foundation is covered by the panels, all you need is a piece of muslin or white cotton. Steam iron the fabric. Cut the foundation fabric 13½" x 11½", which is approximately 4" longer and 4" wider than the image size. This gives you a 2" margin of excess fabric completely around the project.

There are many possibilities for fabrics for the panels. If you want a wild stormy sky, use a mottled hand-dyed fabric for the top sky panel. Use a plain light blue fabric for a calm sky. A variety of green shades works for the hills. I used a hand-dyed marbled fabric. The background is created later. At this point, collect the panel fabrics.

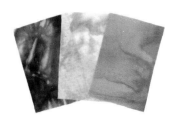

3 Collect Palette Fabrics

Use the list of palette fabrics in the Supply List to gather the fabric colors. You can use more or fewer colors for your project. For future projects you can completely change the color scheme to create a different mood.

4 Select Fusible Web

Choose a fusible web. Read the package directions carefully. I prefer to use Steam-A-Seam 2.

5 Gather Ironing Equipment

Gather your ironing supplies. You need a steam iron and an ironing surface. Take precautions to protect the iron and ironing surface.

6 Pre-Fuse Palette Fabrics

Iron the panel and palette fabrics with a hot steam iron to remove wrinkles and to pre-shrink. Pre-fuse the webbing to the back of the fabrics following the instructions included with the webbing. Peel off the paper liner before cutting any snippets!

7 Trim Palette Fabrics

Clean up the pre-fused fabric by trimming away frayed edges, fabric areas without glue, or excess web hanging over the fabric edges.

Pre-Fusing

For traditional web products, such as Aleene's, Heat N Bond, and Wonder-Under, use the heat of an iron to pre-fuse the fabrics.

For Steam-A-Seam 2, use the pressure of your hand to pre-fuse the fabrics.

8 Determine Depth Order

The depth order for this project is basic. The background panels are the farthest elements and the eagle is the closest. Each of these elements, though, is broken down into a depth order of its own.

The depth order for the background starts with the farthest panel, the sky (1), and goes in order through the hills, from the farthest (2) to the nearest (6).

The eagle is also created in depth order; the back wing (7), the tail (8), foreground wing (9), head (10), beak (11), and eye (12).

9 Create the Background

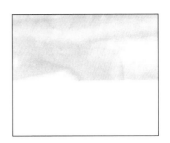

1. Lay the foundation on an ironing board or makeshift board.

2. Place the pre-fused sky fabric on the top portion of the foundation.

3. Cut sweeping hills from the pre-fused hill fabric. Each hill could extend the entire width, or you could layer them in smaller chunks.

4. Start with the farthest hill and lay each hill onto the foundation in depth order until the foundation is covered.

5. Once the panels are in place, set them to the foundation.

10 Cut and Fuse Snippets

Let's start the eagle. Create the eagle in its depth order. Start with large color blocks for the different body parts; then place the different layers of wing, body, and tail feathers; and end with the small details, the beak and eye.

Body Blocks

1. Use the body block pattern below to create base pieces for the body parts. Trace the parts onto the web paper liner. Leave ½" between each piece. Since the webbing is fused to the wrong side of the fabric, whatever you draw on the paper side becomes reversed in the final design. The patterns are flipped for you, so they are ready to trace as drawn.

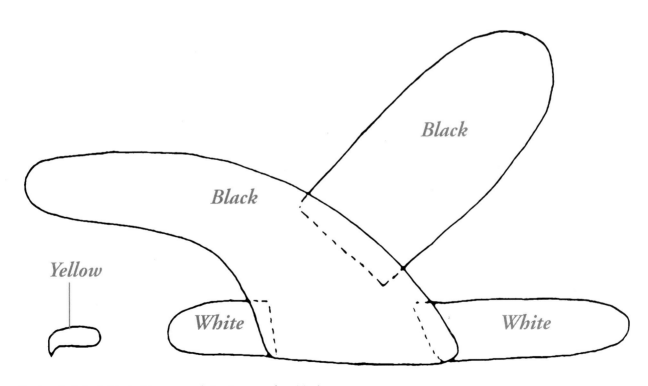

Soaring Eagle body blocks (shown actual size, in reversed position)

2. Cut out each piece, leaving approximately ¼" around the traced lines.

3. Pre-fuse the web pieces to the appropriate fabric colors. Each pattern piece is labeled with the color needed for that piece.

4. Cut the fabric along the traced lines and remove the paper liner. Position all the pieces except the beak onto the foundation. Fuse in place.

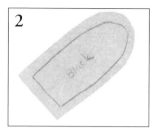
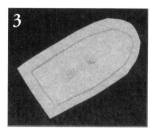
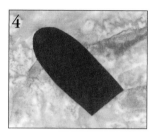

Back Wing

You are ready to place the layers of feather snippets. Do the back wing first:

1. Cut long, thin feather shaped strips from the dark gray and black fabrics. These snippets should be approximately 2" long and ¼" wide.

2. Alternating between the dark gray and black, lay the snippets along the upper and back edges of the wing. (See illustration at left.)

3. Cut feather shaped snippets from the blue gray fabric. These should be approximately 1½" long and ¼" wide. Place a layer of these about an inch inward from the first layer on the upper and back edges of the wing.

4. Fill in the rest of the wing with shorter snippets cut from the medium and light gray fabrics.

5. Check to make sure all the snippets are glue side down. Set the snippet if using traditional web.

Sample back wing snippet shape

Tail Feathers

1. Cut long, thin strips (approximately 3" x ⅛") of white fabric for the tail.

2. Start by placing a layer of these snippets at the very tip of the tail and work inward. If the background color shows through the white tail feathers, add additional layers of white snippets.

3. Place a second layer of white feathers, 1" inward and on top of the previous layer. Let the ends of the feathers overlap the edge of the body. These are covered later with body feathers.

4. Check to make sure all the snippets are glue side down and set the tail snippets if using traditional web.

Sample tail feather snippet shape

Tip

Small scissors, such as Fiskars Micro-tips, are helpful for cutting very small snippets.

Project In Progress—Soaring Eagle

Background panels (sky and hills) in place

Body blocks with back wing feathers added

Tail feather and front wing feathers completed

Head feathers, beak, and eye added

Front Wing

1. For the first layer of feathers, cut black and dark gray snippets, approximately 1½" x ¼".

2. Place the snippets along the top edge of the wing.

3. Cut a single arched snippet for the lead feather on the wing. This creates an upward sweep.

4. Place another layer of black feather snippets about ½" inward from the first layer. Fill in the remaining wing area with short, narrow snippets. Place them so they point upward.

5. Cut several strips of black fabric and place them along the stomach edge to hide the bottom of the wing feathers.

Sample arched lead feather snippet shape

6. Make sure all the snippets are glue side down. Set these snippets in place if using traditional web.

Head

1. Cut thin, short snippets, $\frac{1}{8}$" x $\frac{3}{4}$", from the white fabric. Starting at the neck, place five or six tiny strips of white feathers overlapping the front wing.

2. Work forward, placing layers of white snippets to finish the head.

3. Check that all the pieces are glue side down; these tiny snippets can turn over easily.

Beak and Eye

1. Use the beak pattern and cut a hooked beak piece from canary yellow fabric. It appears backward, but is flipped to the correct direction when placed on the project.

2. Cut a tiny piece of black for the eye.

3. Place the beak and eye on the head. Iron the entire project to permanently adhere all the snippets in place. Use an ironing cloth to protect the white feathers.

11 Review the Project

Stand back about ten feet and review your Snippet Art. Check the overall effect. Are there any areas that seem thin? Are more feathers needed? Add any needed snippets and fuse the entire project one last time.

I usually let a project rest for a few days and then come back for a final critique. Examine your project with a fresh outlook. Add any additional snippets and iron. You are now ready to add embellishments and quilt or frame the project.

12 Embellish

I did not add any embellishments to my design, but perhaps you would like to include some on your project.

13 Finish the Project

Turn back to page 46 of Part II for the different framing options. I framed this project myself. If you decide to frame your own, follow the directions on pages 46–47 to finish the framing process.

14 Clean Up

Wow! You're finished! Wasn't it fun, fast, and easy? Be sure that your iron is clean. Store the unused pieces of pre-fused fabric in a flat position so that they are ready for your next project.

Soaring Eagle quilt by Cindy Walter
Finished Size: 18" x 16"

Turn your *Soaring Eagle* into a small quilted wall hanging by following these easy directions:

Additional supplies needed:

- Black border fabric - ⅛ yard: Cut 4 strips - 1½" x 11"

- Multicolored border fabric - ¼ yard: Cut 2 strips - 3" x 13"

                                                               Cut 2 strips - 3" x 16"

- Cotton batting - craft size (or 20" x 18")

- Backing fabric - 20" x 18"

- Machine quilting supplies: Sewing machine, straight pins, machine quilting thread, darning foot, topstitch needle (90/14 or 100/16)

Create the *Soaring Eagle* following the instructions in this chapter. Once you have permanently set the project with an iron, trim the foundation to 11" x 9". Follow the instructions on page 48 to learn how to attach the borders (using ¼" seam allowance) and finish the project as a quilt.

PROJECT 3 *Italian City*

Finished Size: 24" x 20"   Image Size: 20" x 16"

This project is made entirely with snippets! Using this method makes the design development very flexible. There is the freedom to choose what shape of snippets to cut and where to place them in the design. The directions will guide you through the steps to replicate the design, but then you can customize it in any fashion. A few suggestions: add more trees, a boat, or change the shape or position of the city. I'm sure you will enjoy the freedom and flexibility possible with this project.

Background Style: Snippet Background

This project uses a Snippet Background. The foundation fabric is covered over with many layers of snippets. I love hand-dyed fabrics and have used Shades hand dyed fabrics exclusively in this design. Printed fabrics would give a similar effect.

Project Supply List

- **Foundation Fabric:** ⅔ yard, or a piece measuring 22″ x 18″, muslin or white fabric
- **Palette Fabrics:** Sky—6 shades of light blue (¼ yard total)
  Water—6 shades of dark blue to dark violet (¼ yard total)
  City—6 shades of gold, from yellow to rust (¼ yard total)
  Ground and trees—6 shades of green, light to dark (½ yard total)
  Tree trunk—2 shades of brown (⅛ yard total)
  Ground cover—1 shade of light lavender (scraps)
- **Fusible Web:** 3 yards
- **Scissors**
- **Ironing Supplies:** Iron and ironing board or cardboard ironing surface
- **Framing Supplies:** Mounting board, mat, and frame (mat opening should be approximately 20″ x 16″)

Project Instructions

Each of the following steps is discussed in greater detail in the previous section. If at any time you need a review, turn back to the corresponding step in Part II.

1 Choose a Design

This design was chosen to show a clear, concise example of Snippet Sensations with a Snippet Background. Using snippets exclusively gives the design an impressionistic feel, as if you dabbed the fabrics on with a paint brush.

2 Select a Background Style

Choose a foundation fabric. Since it is covered by snippets, use a piece of muslin or white cotton for the foundation. Steam iron the fabric. Cut the foundation to 22″ x 18″, which is 2″ longer and 2″ wider than the image size. This gives you a 2″ margin of excess fabric completely around the project.

3 Collect Palette Fabrics

Use the list of palette fabrics in the Supply List to gather the fabric colors. You can use more or fewer colors for your project. The marbled effect of hand-dyed fabrics produces a remarkable variation of color.

4 Select Fusible Web

Choose a fusible web. Read the package directions carefully. I prefer to use Steam-A-Seam 2.

5 Gather Ironing Equipment

Gather your ironing supplies. You need a steam iron and an ironing surface. Take precautions to protect the iron and ironing surface.

6 Pre-Fuse Palette Fabrics

Iron the palette fabrics with a hot steam iron to remove wrinkles and to pre-shrink. Pre-fuse the web to the back of the fabrics following the instructions included with the web. Peel off the paper liner before cutting any snippets!

Pre-Fusing

For traditional web products, such as Aleene's, Heat N Bond, and Wonder-Under, use the heat of an iron to pre-fuse the fabrics.

For Steam-A-Seam 2, use the pressure of your hand to pre-fuse the fabrics.

7 Trim Palette Fabrics

Clean up the fabric by trimming away frayed edges, fabric areas without glue, or excess web hanging over the fabric edges.

8 Determine Depth Order

The depth order for this project is twofold. The background is created first: sky (1), water (2), and land (3), in that order. Then the design elements are done in depth order: city (1), ground cover (2), and, finally, the trees (3). Refer to the photographs on page 90 as you create these elements in steps 9 and 10.

Background element placement order

9 Create the Background

If you feel you need a guide to start placing the snippets, lightly draw lines to divide the base into the three background elements; sky, water, and land.

Get a jump start on the background by cutting and distributing large snippets over the sky, water, and land areas.

1. Cut large snippets from each of the "sky" blue fabrics. Cover the sky area with the large blue snippets.

2. Cut long, narrow snippets from each of the water

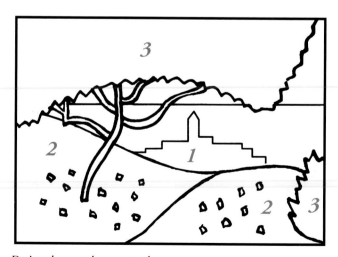

Design element placement order

fabrics and scatter them throughout the water area, parallel to the horizon. The snippets do not have to be uniform in shape.

3. Cut and distribute large snippets of each of the darker greens over the land area. Reserve some of each green to use for the trees and ground cover.

4. Set these snippets in place.

Next, build up the background elements by cutting and setting layers of medium and small sized snippets.

1. For the sky, cut and distribute two or three more layers of medium and small sized snippets until you feel the sky is filled in and no foundation shows through.

2. For the water area, cut and distribute one or two more layers of long, narrow blue snippets until you feel the sea is complete and no foundation shows.

3. For the ground, cut and distribute medium sized snippets of the following:

   • Light greens near the edge of the water.
   • Medium greens through the middle land area.
   • Dark greens across the bottom of the land area.

Continue cutting and distributing green snippets until the ground area is covered.

4. Set the snippets using the appropriate fusing method for your webbing brand.

10 Create the Design Elements

The snippets for some of the design elements are predetermined in shape. The city uses rectangular and square shaped snippets. Long sweeping snippets create realistic tree trunks and branches.

City
1. Cut rectangles and squares of the various golds, from yellow to rust. Reserve a small amount of each fabric for the trees and ground cover.

2. Lay out the pieces, starting from the top and layering the snippets down to the bottom of the city.

3. Check the snippets to see that all have the glue side down.

Land and Ground Cover
1. Place a few green snippets so that they cover the bottom of the city.

2. Further develop the land area by filling in with smaller green snippets.

3. Scatter snippets of lavender and rust on top to give the impression of flowers blossoming on the hillsides. Set the snippets if using traditional web.

"Setting" Snippets

For traditional web, use heat to permanently fuse snippets to the foundation as each layer is completed.

For Steam-A-Seam 2, use light hand pressure to set snippets in place. Iron when ready to permanently fuse them to the foundation. Fuse the project all at once when the entire design is complete.

Large snippets are cut for all three background elements.

Additional layers of medium and small snippets are placed to fill in the gaps.

Add the city. Hills are developed on the land. Some ground cover is added.

Trees are added, then a final sprinkling of ground cover.

Trees

This design has three trees, two large ones in the upper left area and a smaller one in the lower right. Let's start with the large trees.

1. Cut long sweeping trunks and branches from light brown fabric. Sketch the shapes on the paper liner or cut them freehand.

2. Arrange the trunks and branches in the upper left hand corner in a way that fits the balance of your design.

3. Set the pieces.

4. Cut random snippets to create the leaves. Using the reserved pieces of green, start by cutting and placing several dispersed layers of the medium and dark greens along the top of the branches.

5. Finish off with a few accents of lighter green.

6. Follow steps 4 and 5 for the small tree in the right-hand corner.

7. Finish up by adding another sprinkling of green, gold, and lavender ground cover snippets. Permanently fuse all the layers to the foundation.

11 Review the Project

Stand back about ten feet and review your Snippet Art. Check the overall effect. Are there any areas that seem thin? Do any areas of the foundation show through the snippets? Do the trees need more leaves? Add any needed snippets and fuse the entire project one last time.

The photo below shows my original "stopping" place. After reviewing, I felt that another tree and more foliage was needed. Compare this phase with the second "stopping" place on page 90, lower right. With the additions, I am much more satisfied with the overall composition.

12 Embellish

I did not add any embellishments to my design, but perhaps you would like to add some to yours. Do so at this time. If you use glass when you frame, make sure the embellishments will not be pressed down by the glass.

13 Finish the Project

Turn back to page 46 of Part II for the different framing options. I framed this project myself. If you decide to frame yours, follow the directions on pages 46–47 to finish the framing process.

14 Clean Up

Wow! You're finished! Wasn't it fun, fast, and easy? Be sure that your iron is clean. Store the unused pieces of pre-fused fabric in a flat position so that they are ready for your next project. Enjoy!

Italian City *quilt by Cindy Walter*
Finished Size: 32" x 26"

Turn your *Italian City* into a small quilted wall hanging by following these easy directions:

Additional supplies needed:

• Purple border fabric - ¼ yard:

    Cut 2 strips - 1½" x 22"
    Cut 2 strips - 1½" x 20"

• Multicolored border fabric - ½ yard:

    Cut 2 strips - 3½" x 24"
    Cut 2 strips - 3½" x 26"

• Cotton batting - craft size (or 32" x 28")

• Backing fabric - 32" x 28"

• Machine quilting supplies: Sewing machine, straight pins, machine quilting thread, darning foot, topstitch needle (90/14 or 100/16)

Create the *Italian City* following the instructions in this chapter. Once you have permanently set the project with an iron, trim the foundation to 22" x 18". Follow the instructions on page 48 to learn how to attach the borders (using ¼" seam allowance) and finish the project as a quilt.

Suggested Reading

General Quilting

Quilts, Quilts, Quilts!!!
Diana McClun & Laura
Nownes
The Quilt Digest Press
ISBN 0-8442-2616-5

Quilter's Complete Guide
Marianne Fons & Liz Porter
Oxmoor House
ISBN 0-8487-1099-1

The Quilter's Companion
Mimi Dietrich, Donna
Thomas, Joan Hanson, and
Jeana Kimball
That Patchwork Place
ISBN 1-56477-040-0

The New Sampler
Diana Leone
C&T Publishing
ISBN 0-942786-41-6

Machine Quilting

Threadplay
Libby Lehman
That Patchwork Place
ISBN 1-56477-202-0

Machine Quilting Made Easy
by Maurine Noble
That Patchwork Place
ISBN 1-56477-074-5

Decorative Threads
Maurine Noble
That Patchwork Place

Heirloom Machine Quilting
Harriet Hargrave
C&T Publishing
ISBN 0-914881-33-7

Supply Sources

~Alaska Dyeworks
100% Cotton
Hand Dyed Fabric
300 W. Swanson, #101
Wasilla, AK 99654
(800) 478-1755

~Creative Beginnings
Decorative Charms
475 Morro Bay Blvd.
Morro Bay, CA 93442

Eddie's Quilting Bee
264 Castro St.
Mountain View, CA 94041
(888) QUILTER

~Fiskars, Inc.
Softouch™ Micro-tip scissors
Softouch™ Multi-purpose scissors
7811 West Stewart Ave.
Wausau, WI 54401

Freudenberg Nonwovens
Pellon Division
Wonder-Under™ Transfer Web
119 W. 40th St.
New York, NY 10018

~Hoffman California-
International
Hoffman Fabrics
25792 Obrero Drive
Misson Viejo, CA 92691-3140

~Monarch/Northcott Fabrics
229 W. 36th St.
New York, NY 10018
(212) 563-0450

Prym Dritz Corp.
Iron-off® Hot Iron Cleaner
PO Box 2009
Spartanburg, SC 29304

Shades Inc. Hand Dyed Textiles
Hand Dyed Fabric
585 Cobb Pkwy. S.
The Nynn Complex, Studio "O"
Marietta, GA 30062-8202
(800) 783-3933

~Therm O Web, Inc.
Heat N Bond Iron-on Adhesive
Consumer Products Division
770 Glenn Ave.
Wheeling, IL 60090

~The Warm Company
Steam-A-Seam 2® Double Stick
Web
Warm & Natural® Batting
954 E. Union St.
Seattle, WA 98122

~Our thanks to these companies, who have generously donated products used to create some of the beautiful pieces in this book.

94

More Original Ideas From Cindy Walter

More Snippet Sensations

by Cindy Walter

Thousands of people around the world have let their creativity soar with Cindy Walter's revolu-

tionary, contemporary Snippet Sensations technique, where small "snippets" of fabric and fusible web are used to "paint" on fabric. This follow-up to the award-winning Snippet Sensations explores applications for Snippet-inspired quilts and wearables, as well as expanded instructions for free-motion machine quilting. As an added bonus, there is a gallery that showcases breathtaking Snippet quilts and 20 step-by-step projects.

Softcover • 8-1/4 x 10-7/8 • 112 pages
75 color photos
Item# SNIP2 • $19.95

Cindy Walter's Snippets Sensations Christmas Celebration

by Cindy Walter

Creating unique and festive decorations for the Christmas season has never been so easy and exciting. Author Cindy Walter guides you through 10 holiday projects, including wreaths, snowmen, and a Christmas tree, using her revolu-

tionary snippet technique-where "snippets" of fabric and fusible webbing are used to "paint" on fabric. Includes step-by-step instructions and detailed illustrations.

Softcover • 8-1/4 x 10-7/8 • 24 pages
20+ color photos
Item# HSNIP • $7.95

Cindy Walter's Snippet Sensations Bouquets

by Cindy Walter

Creating art with fabric has never been so fun

and easy! In Cindy Walter's new book you'll be introduced to her revolutionary Snippet Sensations technique, where "snippets" of fabric and fusible web are used to "paint" on fabric. You'll then be guided with step-by-step

instructions through 10 stunning floral projects that can be quilted, including a sunflower quilt.

Softcover • 8-1/4 x 10-7/8 • 24 pages
30 color photos
Item# SNBQT • $7.95

Fine Hand Quilting

2nd Edition

by Diana Leone & Cindy Walter

The art of hand quilting is given the royal treat-

ment in this completely revised second edition of the most respected book on the topic. World-renown authors and teachers Diana Leone and Cindy Walter have tested all of the latest tools and materials on the market, provided tried-and-true tech-

niques so you can create even stitches, and included three projects to get you started right away! This full-color update also has tips from quilting pros, a special section on "How to Quilt This Quilt," and a gallery of gorgeous, inspirational quilts.

Softcover • 8-1/4 x 10-7/8 • 112 pages
150 color photos
Item# FHQU • $19.95

Attic Windows

Quilts With a View, 2nd Edition

by Diana Leone & Cindy Walter

Attic Windows is a timeless technique for quil-

ters of all ages and skill levels to use their imagination, creativity, and favorite motif fabrics. Now in full color, this comprehensive volume contains a gallery of more than 50 inspiring Attic Window quilts, information on selecting fabrics,

tips on how to use colors effectively, and numerous exercises to help you plan a one-of-a-kind quilt. Diana Leone is the author of such highly regarded books as Fine Hand Quilting, while Cindy Walter is the creator of the Snippet Sensations technique and author of the award-winning book of the same name.

Softcover • 8-1/4 x 10-7/8 • 96 pages
20 illustrations • 100 color photos
Item# ATWI • $19.95

The Basic Guide to Dyeing and Painting Fabric

by Cindy Walter & Jennifer Priestly

Now you can learn how to make your own one-of-a-kind hand-painted and -dyed fabrics with this exciting new book! You'll find 10 projects for dyeing and painting quilts, wearables, purses, pillows and more, along with step-by-step instructions. You'll love how these easy tech-

niques can brighten up your life!

Softcover • 8-1/4 x 10-7/8 • 112 pages
200 color photos
Item# FTDF • $19.95

Enhance Your Creativity with Help from the Professionals

The Magic of Crazy Quilting
A Complete Resource For Embellished Quilting
by J. Marsha Michler

This book is a glorious gallery of exquisite quilts that delight the eye and inspire the hands. It guides you in creating a crazy quilt from start to finish with an outstanding collection of embellishment techniques, piecing methods, embroidery stitch variations, combinations and patterns for pieced fan embroideries.
Softcover • 8-1/4 x 10-7/8 • 144 pages
150 photos & 250 illustrations
MCQ • $21.95

Adventures with Polarfleece
A Sewing Expedition
by Nancy Cornwell

Nancy Cornwell will lead you on a sewing expedition. Explore and discover endless project possibilities for the entire family. Sew a collection of 15 projects for play, work, fashion, comfort and warmth. The heart of a fallen-away sewer will soon be recaptured and new sewers will be intrigued and inspired.
Softcover • 8-1/2 x 11 • 160 pages
200 color photos • 150 color illustrations
AWPF • $19.95

More Polarfleece® Adventures
by Nancy Cornwell
Add designer touches to fleece with cutwork, sculpturing, appliqué, pintucking, fancy edge finishes, designer buttonholes, and machine embroidery.

Start off with a quick refresher course and end with a chapter filled with fun fleece projects. In between, you'll find a new world of sewing loaded with templates and patterns for the designs featured.
Softcover • 8-1/4 x 10-7/8 • 160 pages
200 color photos
Item# AWPF2 • $19.95

Fast-Folded Flowers
Timesaving Techniques for a Quilted Bouquet
by Laura Farson

Who can resist a bouquet of beautiful flowers, especially when they're three-dimensional quilted designs? Learn 12 quick and easy techniques for flower petal quilt blocks that can be used to create quilts, lap robes, baby blankets, trivet covers potholders and home décor items. Easy to understand instructions for 17 projects that utilize a sewing machine and no handwork offer quick, eye-appealing results. Quilters, crafters and sewers of all skill levels will enjoy creating these delightful quilted bouquets.
Softcover • 8-1/4 x 10-7/8 • 128 pages
175 color photos & illustrations
Item# FFFQT • $21.95

Quick Quilted Miniatures
by Darlene Zimmerman
Create miniature quilts simply and quickly using the tips and techniques provided in this

book. The author leads you through 38 miniature quilt designs. Colors and designs mimic décor, holidays and occasions occurring throughout the year. Featuring 40 color photographs and 140 illustrations, the book offers basic cutting and assembly information, step-by-step instructions, and tips on choosing and organizing fabric, drafting your own designs and appliqué basics.
Softcover • 8-1/4 x 10-7/8 • 128 pages
40 color photos & 140 illustrations
Item# QQM • $21.95

Raw Edge Appliqué
by Jodie Davis
Imagine making a Dresden Plate minus fussy needle-turn appliqué or an Orange Peel without

matching a curve-sound like a dream? Well, with Jodie Davis' new book, it's a reality! You'll find 10 fun and fast quilt projects that eliminate hours of pinning and matching by using a straight machine stitch. The raw edges are left exposed to become slightly frayed as the quilt is loved, washed and dried-and then loved some more. Features easy-to-follow instructions, detailed illustrations and gorgeous photos of the finished quilts.
Softcover • 8-1/4 x 10-7/8 • 96 pages
20 color photos
Item# FEQ • $19.95